STRUCTURED TUTORING

The Instructional Design Library

Volume 34

STRUCTURED TUTORING

Grant Von Harrison
Brigham Young University

Ronald Edward Guymon
Brigham Young University

Danny G. Langdon
Series Editor

Educational Technology Publications
Englewood Cliffs, New Jersey 07632

Library of Congress Cataloging in Publication Data

Harrison, Grant Von.
Structured tutoring.

(The Instructional design library; v. 34)
Bibliography: p.
1. Tutors and tutoring. I. Guymon, Ronald Edward,
joint author. II. Title. III. Series: Instructional
design library; v. 34.
LC41.H3   371.39'4   79-23035
ISBN 0-87778-154-0

Printed in the United States of America.

Library of Congress Catalog Card Number:
79-23035.

International Standard Book Number:
0-87778-154-0.

First Printing: March, 1980.

FOREWORD

The controversy that sometimes prevails over just how "structured" learning should be will never subside, nor should it. Those against structure see it in a negative outcome of inhibiting free thinking and indeed the translation of what is learned to more generalizable thoughts and actions. This has often been the critical comment aimed at any instructional design which is highly programmed. Perhaps the answer is as simple as recognizing that there is a place for structure and nonstructure (really, semi-structure) in meeting learning needs.

There is a place for instructional designs that are highly (not just somewhat, one-half, or three quarters) structured. Designs that are highly structured have probably proven more than others that they are effective and efficient for guiding student learning. The fact that they are structured makes it easier to scrutinize them. The proof of their value, like that of any design, is that they produce learning. Such is the case with Structured Tutoring.

Anyone involved in tutoring or seriously thinking about implementing it will find this book highly useful. The step-by-step, detail-laden approach taken by the authors not only explains the design but also provides a structure and convenient set of aids for implementation.

Danny G. Langdon
Series Editor

PREFACE

As tutoring programs of various types receive attention as possible solutions to modern educational problems, it becomes necessary to evaluate them in terms of their benefits to the students involved. Recent research has shown that tutoring *per se* is not necessarily beneficial. However, research and experimentation have demonstrated that tutoring is effective when tutors are trained to follow specified principles of learning. This book examines one such tutoring model, that has become known as Structured Tutoring. In Chapter I, "Use," the research concerning tutoring systems in general is presented and the evolution of the Structured Tutoring model is discussed.

The Structured Tutoring model is characterized by (1) a precise tutor-student relationship and (2) highly structured instructional materials. To ensure an effective tutor-student relationship, tutors must be trained so that they are totally conversant with both general tutoring techniques and procedures. General procedures, such as establishing and maintaining rapport with the student, avoiding "no" as a response, clarifying expectations, creating opportunities for success, etc., are discussed in Chapter II, "Operational Description."

Specific tutoring techniques and procedures are integrally related to the nature of the desired instructional objectives. Generally speaking, however, specific tutoring techniques and procedures can be categorized into five basic steps: (1) preassess the student's present ability; (2) prepare to tutor the student; (3) tutor the student using the proper tutoring techniques and procedures; (4) maintain the appropriate records; and (5) review the student's progress. In Chapter III, "Design Format," the five steps of the Structured Tutoring model are discussed in detail as they apply to stimulus-response learning tasks.

Chapter IV, "Outcomes," takes a brief look at the results of the Structured Tutoring model. Benefits to the tutors as well as to the students who have received the tutoring are discussed.

For the reader intending to apply the Structured Tutoring model, a Developmental Guide is provided in Chapter V.

In Chapter VI, "Resources," the reader is provided with a current list of the various manuals and instructional systems which are based on the Structured Tutoring model as it is applied to a variety of learning tasks.

G.V.H.
R.E.G.

CONTENTS

ABSTRACT

STRUCTURED TUTORING

In this book, the authors challenge the prevailing notion that tutoring *per se* results in significant gains and benefits to tutors and students. Research demonstrates, however, that when tutors are trained to follow specified principles of learning, both tutors and students benefit significantly. The authors describe the evolution of the Structured Tutoring model and contrast this model with traditional tutoring techniques. The five basic components of the Structured Tutoring model are discussed in detail as they apply to stimulus-response learning tasks. The reader is also given a list of various instructional systems based on the Structured Tutoring model as it is applied to a variety of learning tasks.

STRUCTURED TUTORING

I.

USE

Many of history's honored teachers were tutors (e.g., Socrates, Plato, Confucius, Tao): they engaged students one at a time in profitable dialogue. An examination of journals and conference papers shows that tutoring is once again being considered a hopeful model of instruction for solving many of the ills of education. The tutoring programs range from the more media-oriented, teacher-absent approaches, such as programmed instruction and audio-tutorial systems (Postleth-wait, Novak, and Murray, 1969), to programs in which tutors (students or adults) work with learners on a one-to-one situation (Harrison, 1969; Weingarten, Hungerland, and Brennan, 1972). Despite the obvious differences in these approaches, the claims are much the same—the tutored students will benefit from being tutored.

The Problem: The Need for a Clearer Definition of Tutoring

Tutoring is commonly thought of as an informal interaction between a tutor and a student in which skills or information are transferred. Often there is a vague conception of the *process* which is involved in the transfer because this process is seldom defined. Even though the idea of providing students individualized help by having someone tutor them has been a fairly common practice for years, it has only been recently that questions associated with tutoring have been investigated empirically. For example, it is repeatedly asserted that tutoring (and the term is used here in its vaguest sense) results in significant gains and benefits to the tutors as well as the students. However, most of the "evidence" for this assertion consists only of anecdotal accounts. Indeed, a literature search (Harrison, 1969) turned up no empirical evidence to support this assertion as of 1967, except for a study by Ellson (1967) in which adults were used as tutors.

A survey of major tutorial programs in 1968 (Thelen, 1968) brought a very interesting point to light. In over 80 percent of the programs reviewed, the rationale for establishing a tutorial program was the assumed benefits for the tutor, *not* the benefits for the student being tutored. Yet, in no instance was any empirical data collected to substantiate the assumed benefits. Furthermore, it is unfortunate that in only a few instances was any effort made to collect data to assess what benefits, if any, the students being tutored were realizing.

As is the case with many innovations adopted by educators, sketchy anecdotal data are all that are needed to make a sweeping generalization that the innovation is producing significant results.

In 1972, Bright reported the results of a study made in 32 schools boasting formidable reputations for individualized instruction. Bright wanted to know whether the instruction taking place at these schools was indeed "individualized." One major source of information in the investigation was a simple survey that posed to teachers the following three questions:

1. Do you know where each student is in relation to a predetermined sequence?
2. Do you know what skills each student is working on now?
3. Do you know what skills each student has mastered?

The results of the study were not very encouraging. According to Bright's criteria, only two of the schools surveyed were providing instruction that was actually "individualized" (Bright, 1972).

However, even if all 32 schools surveyed had met criteria for individualized instruction, there would still be no guarantee that the needs of low-achievers were being met.

Most forms of individualized instruction demand that students work independently, read at grade level, pace themselves, and demonstrate a high degree of self-discipline and motivation. These demands are usually too rigorous for low-achievers with poor study habits, lack of self-confidence, low motivation, poor self-discipline, short attention span, or limited reading skills.

For these reasons, both the "cafeteria" model, allowing low-achievers to pick and choose their own subject matter and learning activities, and the "paddle-your-own-canoe" approach, allowing them to pace themselves, usually fail to meet the needs of low-achieving students. But of all the forms of "individualized" instruction, the most *inappropriate,* especially for primary grade low-achievers, are those employing programmed texts or workbooks. Why? Because these programs rely on printed materials that require low-achievers to apply reading skills that they very often do not possess.

Unless the specific needs of students are diagnosed, unless learning activities are prescribed on the basis of diagnosis, and unless means to compensate for lack of reading skills, motivation, etc., are provided, individualized instruction will fail to meet the needs of low-achievers.

Carroll (1964) has argued that the quality of instruction improves when the presentation and explanation of materials, and the ordering of task elements, are tailored for the given student. Furthermore, research (Blank and Solomon, 1969; Congrave, 1965; Harrison, 1967) has shown that low-achieving students will not learn consistently unless they are involved in a teaching-learning process that is highly structured and sensitive to their personal needs. Could we go a step further and say that the quality of instruction should be evaluated in light of the progress of students having difficulties rather than on the progress of random groups of learners? Bateman (1969) says yes. In commenting on this consideration, she made the following statement:

> The normal child can achieve up to grade level even if we never do anything right in the classroom. He will learn in spite of us; but the child with learning disabilities will not; and it is through him that we are going to learn about learning. (p. ii)

So far it has not been possible to create a highly sensitive, personal, and structured learning environment without employing some kind of tutorial approach. A study by Blank and Solomon (1969) revealed that a highly structured tutorial model helped low-achievers make significant progress, but the same model failed to do so when the tutoring was not highly structured.

Bloom (1971) expressed the same idea in his article, "Learning for Mastery." Bloom pointed out that most students would master given subjects if they had good tutors. According to Bloom, a good tutor:

> ... must be skillful in detecting the points of difficulty in the student's learning, and should help him in such a way as to free the student from continued dependence on him ... [and] tutoring should be available to students as they need it. (p. 49)

In various articles by Harrison (e.g., "Tutoring: A Remedy Reconsidered"), the same points have been stressed. Research over the past eight years has shown that a low-achiever will realize optimal learning progress only when he or she has access to an individual tutor (a) whose role is highly structured, (b) who knows how to employ proven psychological principles of learning, and (c) who knows how to use appropriate instructional materials.

The Solution: Structured Tutoring

In a series of experiments conducted over the past decade (Harrison, 1967, 1968, 1969, 1971, 1972), several pertinent findings have been substantiated. In essence, the findings have shown that tutoring *per se* does not benefit students in most instances. In sharp contrast, it has been demonstrated that if tutoring is approached in a highly structured way, students can benefit a great deal from tutoring. This particular approach to tutoring, which is espoused by the authors, has become known as *Structured Tutoring*. The authors are convinced that any successful tutoring programs will involve most, if not all, of the elements described in the Structured Tutoring model.

The procedures and techniques involved in Structured Tutoring represent, to some extent, principles of learning which have been identified primarily with programmed instruction. In a sense, Structured Tutoring is an extension of programmed instruction, in which the tutorial procedures are carefully prescribed and conform to basic tenets of programmed instruction. However, Structured Tutoring opens up several new dimensions of instruction. It is the first form of individualized instruction capable of accurately monitoring oral response. It is also the first form of individualized instruction capable of monitoring the student's behavior while he or she attempts to solve a problem. Structured Tutoring provides a degree of flexibility with instruction that cannot be duplicated with computers. Tutoring techniques and procedures are identified which allow for maximum sensitivity to the individual learning characteristics of the student being tutored so as to maximize learning gains.

Nature of Subject Matter and Audience Addressed
by the Structured Tutoring Model

Structured Tutoring is a teaching technique rather than a set of materials, so that the subject matter taught can be determined entirely by the curricular requirements of the school system in which it is used. Research indicates that this type of tutoring has great potential for individualizing instruction at all grade levels, and it could very possibly provide the answer to the ever-pressing problem of effectively adapting instruction at the primary grade level to individual differences.

In one of his earliest papers, Skinner (1958) compared the potential of programmed learning with a private tutor. In this comparison, several characteristics of a good tutor are emphasized. For example, a good tutor (a) causes a constant interchange, (b) induces sustained activity, (c) assures that the student is always busy, (d) insists that a point be thoroughly understood before the student moves on, (e) presents just that material for which the student is ready, (f) helps the student come up with the right answer, and (g) reinforces the student for every correct response.

Thus far, programmed instruction has not lived up to Skinner's expectations, and it is becoming obvious that tutoring *per se* does not automatically result in the type of interaction he described. Also, most forms of programmed instruction are heavily dependent on reading ability and the ability to work independently, which has made it extremely difficult to write programs for non-reading students or for students who for one reason or another have difficulty working independently. Based on existing research, it would appear that Structured Tutoring is a possible means of achieving the type of interaction between a learner and instructional material Skinner felt was necessary for effective learning.

The Structured Tutoring model can be utilized to teach any objective that can be evaluated empirically. However, the authors are of the opinion that only high-priority objectives warrant the intense individualized instruction that Structured Tutoring provides. Secondly, the authors suggest that this form of instruction be used as a complement to, rather than as a substitute for, the total instruction a student receives during the day.

Even though the Structured Tutoring model was originally designed to cope with the unique learning characteristics of low-achieving primary grade children who are considered high risks in terms of probability of failure, Structured Tutoring can be used to teach most objectives not readily attained by students generally at any grade level.

For example, instructional materials have been developed and validated following the Structured Tutoring model which effectively transfer basic reading and mathematics skills. In addition, instructional materials have been developed in the areas of creative writing and also second language acquisition.

Whereas the prime focus of the authors' early research was directed to devising Structured Tutoring procedures that would consistently enhance the probability of success for low-achieving primary grade children, in recent years the authors have conducted extensive research dealing with other populations (junior high, high school, and university students, as well as other adults).

Summary

As tutoring programs of various types receive attention as possible solutions to modern educational problems, it becomes necessary to evaluate them in terms of their benefits to the students involved. Recent research has shown that tutoring *per se* is not necessarily beneficial—that unsystematic approaches to tutoring in which tutors are untrained and methods are not prescribed are not the panaceas they attempt to be. However, further research and experimentation has demonstrated the effectiveness of Structured Tutoring. Structured Tutoring systems have been developed which effectively train tutors in various content areas and which address audiences representing various age groups.

References

Bateman, B. *A Remedial Diagnostic Handbook for Children with Learning Disabilities.* Edinburg, Texas: Region One Education Service Center, 1969.

Blank, M., and F. Solomon. How Shall the Disadvantaged Be Taught? *Child Development,* 1969, *40,* 47-61.

Bloom, B.S., J.T. Hastings, and G.F. Madaus. Learning for Mastery. Chapter 3. *Handbook on Formative and Summative Evaluation of Student Learning.* New York: McGraw-Hill, 1971.

Bright, L. *Description of a Contingency Management System.* Speech given at Brigham Young University, Provo, Utah, Summer 1972.

Carroll, J. A Model of School Learning. *Teachers College Record,* 1964, *64*(8), 723-733.

Congrave, W.J. Independent Learning. *North Central Association Quarterly,* 1965, *40,* 222-228.

Ehrle, E.B. Avoiding the Audio-Tutorial Mistake. *Bioscience,* 1970, *20,* p. 103.

Ellson, D.G. *Results of Tutorial Project.* Indianapolis: Indianapolis Public Schools, 1967.

Harrison, G.V. Training Students to Tutor. Technical Memorandum 3686/000/00. Santa Monica, California: System Development Corporation, 1967.

Harrison, G.V. Training Students to Tutor. A proposal submitted to the University of California at Los Angeles, July 1968.

Harrison, G.V. The Effects of Trained and Untrained Student Tutors on the Criterion Performance of Disadvantaged First-Graders. Paper presented at the California Educational Research Association Annual Meeting, Los Angeles, California, March 1969.

Harrison, G.V. Training Students to Tutor. Paper submitted to the Committee on Diagnostic Reading Tests, Inc., for inclusion in the Workshop in Reading Research, Las Vegas, Nevada, April 1969.

Harrison, G.V. An Individualized Teaching Strategy for Culturally Deprived Pupils: A Systems Approach to Intergrade Tutoring. Paper presented at the annual convention of the National Society for Programmed Instruction, Washington, D.C., April 3-12, 1969.

Harrison, G.V. The Effect of Professional and Nonprofessional Trainers Using Prescribed Training Procedures on the Performance of Uppergrade Elementary Student Tutors. Doctoral dissertation, University of California at Los Angeles, 1969.

Harrison, G.V. The Empirical Validation of Specified Tutorial Procedures. Provo, Utah: Brigham Young University, 1969.

Harrison, G.V. Structured Tutoring. Paper presented at the annual convention of the National Society for Programmed Instruction, Rochester, New York, March 31-April 3, 1971.

Harrison, G.V. An Introspection to a Student Tutoring Program. *Working Paper No. 23.* Provo, Utah: Brigham Young University, Department of Instructional Research and Development, 1971.

Harrison, G.V. Tutorial Project for Illiterate Adults. Final Report. Submitted to the Director of the Adult Education Program in the Provo School District, Provo, Utah, 1971.

Harrison, G.V. Instructional Managers: The Key to More Effective Beginning Reading Instruction. Paper presented at the California Educational Research Association Annual Meeting, San Jose, California, November 8, 1972.

Harrison, G.V. Tutoring: A Remedy Reconsidered. *Improving Human Performance: A Research Quarterly,* 1972, *1*(4), 1-5.

Harrison, G.V., and V. Brimley. The Use of Structured Tutoring Techniques in Teaching Low-Achieving Six-Year-

Olds to Read. Paper presented at the American Educational Research Association Annual Meeting, New York City, February 3-7, 1971.

Harrison, G.V., and A.M. Cohen. Empirical Validation of Tutor Training Procedures. September 1969.

Harrison, G.V., W. Nelson, and L. Tregaskis. The Use of a Structured Tutorial Reading Program in Teaching Non-Reading Second-Graders in Title I Schools to Read. Paper presented at the American Educational Research Association's Annual Meeting, Chicago, Illinois, April 3-7, 1972.

Husband, D.D. The Audio-Tutorial System. *Audio-Visual Instruction,* 1970, *15,* 34-35.

Lippitt, P., and J.E. Lohman. Cross-Age Relationships: An Educational Resource. *Children,* 1965, *12,* 113-117.

Niedermeyer, F.C. The Effects of Training on the Instructional Behaviors of Student Tutors. Southwest Regional Laboratory Research Memorandum, March 30, 1969.

Niedermeyer, F.C., and P. Ellis. Remedial Reading Instruction by Trained Pupil Tutors. *The Elementary School Journal,* 1971, *71*(7), 400-405.

Postlethwait, S.N. The Use of Audio-Tape for a Multifaceted Approach to Teaching Botany. *American Journal of Botany,* 1962, *49,* p. 681.

Postlethwait, S.N. A Systems Approach to Botany. *Audio-Visual Instruction,* 1963, *8,* 234-244.

Postlethwait, S.N. Independent Study: An Audio-Tutorial Approach. *Current Issues in Higher Education.* Proceeding, 19th Annual National Conference on Higher Education, 1964, 134-135.

Postlethwait, S.N. The Audio-Tutorial Approach: Language Teaching Method Adapted to Science Lab Course at Purdue. *Minnemath Reports,* 1964, *2,* 3-10.

Postlethwait, S.N. Course Organization for Individualized Instruction. *CUEBA News,* 1965, *1*(3), 1-2.

Postlethwait, S.N. Teaching Tools and Techniques: An

Audio-Tutorial Approach to Teaching. *Pacific Speech,* 1967, *1*(40).

Postlethwait, S.N., J.D. Novak, and H.T. Murray, Jr. *The Audio-Tutorial Approach to Learning Through Independent Study and Integrated Experiences.* Minneapolis: Burgess Publishing Co., 1969.

Skinner, B.F. Teaching Machines. *Science,* 1958, 128 (3330), 971.

Syrocki, J., C. Thomas, and G.C. Fairchild. The Audio-Video Tutorial Program. *American Biological Teachers,* 1969, *39*(2), p. 91.

Thelen, H.A. (Ed.) *Learning by Teaching.* (2nd ed.) Conference on the Helping Relationship in the Classroom, University of Chicago, July 1968.

Weingarten, K., J.E. Hungerland, and M.F. Brennan. Development and Implementation of a Quality-Assured Peer-Instructional Model. Human Resources Research Organization Technical Report, April 1972.

II.

OPERATIONAL DESCRIPTION

As the name implies, the Structured Tutoring model is characterized by a very precise tutor-student relationship. Research has repeatedly demonstrated that unless tutors are trained, there is no guarantee that students will benefit from tutorial instruction. The tutoring relationship and the use of instructional materials are relatively complex tasks which cannot be left to chance. In order to ensure that the tutoring relationship is what it ought to be, it is necessary that tutors be trained in specific techniques and procedures, such as how to achieve rapport and how to clarify the desired response for the learner. The focus of training programs in tutor-learner relationships must allow tutors to *practice* the actual behaviors and procedures rather than merely to talk about them. For example, research (Harrison, 1967; Niedermeyer, 1969) has shown that, generally, tutors do not spontaneously do things that will enhance learning, such as reinforcing the learner for success or insisting that a given point be thoroughly understood before allowing the learner to progress in a sequence. Research has also shown that the effectiveness of tutoring is primarily dependent on the way the tutor interacts with the learner, and that unless this interaction is specified and controlled by appropriate training and/or highly structured tutor manuals, there seems to be little value in having students tutor other students. If anything, the effect may be negative. There has been

15

repeated evidence of undesirable behavior by tutors who are not trained to avoid certain authoritarian patterns. For example, untrained tutors are often unduly stern and tend to punish learners while identifying their incorrect responses.

Training techniques and procedures for Structured Tutoring fall into the following four categories, which will be discussed later in detail: (1) *General:* Including how to establish and maintain a good rapport with the learner, how to use established psychological principles of learning, and how to ensure that a learner has mastered a particular step in a sequence. (2) *Material Specific:* Including prescriptions for training tutors to use materials once they are selected or prepared and for developing procedures which are responsive to the learner's interaction with the materials. (3) *Task Specific:* Including the training which must focus on techniques and procedures that are unique to the particular instructional objectives the tutors are dealing with. For example, the training a tutor would receive relative to teaching a learner to blend sounds would be markedly different from the training involved when teaching a learner to solve a specific type of math problem. (4) *Record Keeping:* Including general aspects of record keeping as well as other aspects unique to the instructional objectives being dealt with. In either case, careful records must be kept to guide decisions, such as when to move on, to repeat, or to skip to other materials.

Procedures and Tutoring Techniques: General

Over the past several years, the authors have reviewed the literature as well as conducted original research to determine general procedures and tutoring techniques which tend to enhance the tutoring relationship. It should be noted that while the following list of general procedures and techniques is representative of the authors' research conducted thus far, the list is by no means complete. It is anticipated that future research will yield a more complete list.

I. Establish and Maintain Rapport with the Student

The student who has encountered failure throughout his or her academic career is likely to be defensive about academic problems. This may take several guises, including apathy, belligerence, or clowning; there are as many variations as there are students. It is very important that the tutor take steps to establish and maintain rapport with the student he or she is tutoring. The manner in which this is accomplished will vary from student to student, but there are some basic principles that apply for most students.

Generally, the following techniques will assist the tutor in establishing rapport with the student.

- Express empathy. For example, if the tutor had a lack of interest in high school, had poor study habits, or had difficulty with the same course, he or she should tell the student about it and what he or she did to solve the problem. In other words, the tutor should let the student know that he or she had academic problems, too.

- Ask questions about the things the student identifies with (school teams, a particular major league basketball team, or a particular professional athlete, etc.).

- Talk about things that both the tutor and the student have a common interest in—cars, dancing, sports, hobbies.

- Be candid and frank. If in an effort to establish and maintain rapport with the student, the tutor becomes patronizing or insincere, the effort to establish rapport will have a negative effect instead of a positive one.

- Recognize the student's reactions to the tutoring and give credence to them ("Well, Tim, you didn't seem to be very excited about that activity. I can understand that; I'll try something different the next time we meet.").

Each time the tutor meets with the student, he or she should ask a few questions about things the student has been doing or the things in which the student has a special interest before beginning tutoring. If the tutor will remember to follow these simple suggestions when tutoring a student, he or she will generally be successful in gaining the confidence of the student. The tutor must also learn to be sensitive to the temperament and disposition of the person he or she is assigned to tutor, or he or she will be unsuccessful. The trick for the tutor to remember is to get cues from the student. For example, if the student is sullen and indifferent, the worst thing the tutor could do would be to be extremely enthusiastic about the tutoring and adopt the attitude of "Aren't we going to have fun!" If the student responds to the tutor somewhat indifferently, the tutor should rely more on topics of discussion to break down the barriers.

As a rule, the tutor should spend about five minutes the first time he or she meets with the student for the purpose of establishing rapport. In each subsequent session, the tutor should spend about one minute with the intent of maintaining or building rapport with the student.

The tutor should not make the mistake of letting large segments of the tutoring session succumb to the tendency of merely "shop talk" in lieu of the task at hand as it relates to a particular academic subject area. The role of the tutor is not that of a counselor. The primary goal of the tutor should be the academic success of the student.

II. Avoid Saying "No"

In a tutorial relationship, a student is going to make numerous responses. These responses can be either oral or written. In our American society, we have a tendency to habitually punish by always saying "no" or "that is wrong" when someone answers or performs incorrectly. For this reason, the tutor has the responsibility to avoid saying "no," "that's wrong," or other forms of negative feedback when the student gives an incorrect response. If the tutor fails to avoid saying "no" or "that is wrong," etc., when he or she is tutoring a student, there will be an adverse effect on the student's confidence and his or her overall initiative.

The tutor has the responsibility to provide the student honest feedback regarding his or her incorrect responses without saying "no" or "that is wrong." This can be accomplished in a variety of ways. For example, the tutor can simply tell the student what the correct answer is or show him or her how to solve a particular problem. Or, the tutor can specifically identify those aspects of the student's responses that are correct and those areas where he or she became confused or performed improperly. As simple as this particular point may seem on the surface, it is extremely critical in a tutorial relationship.

III. Consistently Praise and Encourage the Student

Each time the student responds correctly or is able to do whatever is expected in terms of the academic subject, the tutor should say things to provide him or her positive feedback ("Very good!" "That's right." "You're doing extremely well."). It is important that the tutor use variety in his or her praise, and more importantly, speak with feeling when he or she provides praise.

The tutor should make it a point to accentuate the praise when the student is able to master something that has been particularly difficult for him or her. The strength of verbal praise is contingent upon consistency, sincerity, variety, and appropriate accentuation. In praising the student, the tutor should say things to generally encourage him or her from time to time ("You have really made a lot of progress over the last two weeks.").

IV. Sit at the Side of the Student

When the tutor is working with a student, it is very important that the tutor sit at the side of the student and place the instructional materials on the table in front of both the tutor and the student. The tutor should not sit on the opposite side of the table or across the room when he or she is working with a student (see Figure 1).

V. Work Consistently with the Student

The effectiveness of the tutoring techniques and procedures depends upon the frequency and consistency of the tutoring sessions. A general guideline to follow is that tutoring sessions should take place a minimum of three times per week, at 15 to 60 minutes per session, depending on the attention span of the student and the nature of the task. Generally, three 20-minute tutoring sessions per week will consistently provide better results than one 60-minute session per week, or even two 30-minute sessions per week. Another guideline is that the tutoring session should end while the student's affect is positive and before it starts to decline (see Figure 2). Every effort should be taken to ensure that each tutoring session is a very positive experience for the student. Clearly, the student's attention span and interest in the instructional task are key factors in determining the length of each tutoring session.

VI. Give Special Recognition for Achievement

Special recognition can be given in a variety of ways. Here are some specific examples that tutors have devised:

1. Tell someone (peers, parents, teacher, spouse) in front of the student how well he or she is doing and mention specific concepts, rules, ideas, etc., that he or she has learned.
2. Give the student special privileges wherever appropriate (getting out of school early, playing a game such

Figure 1

Correct and Incorrect Positions of Student and Tutor

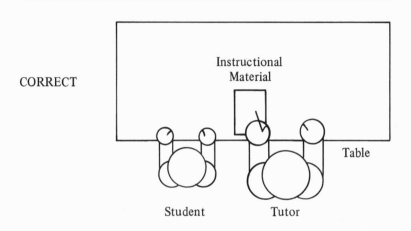

CORRECT

Instructional Material

Table

Student   Tutor

NOTE: Do not face the student when tutoring.

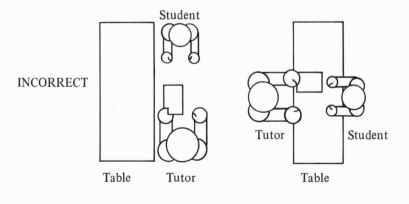

INCORRECT

Student

Table   Tutor

Tutor   Student

Table

Figure 2

Curve Showing When a Tutoring Session Should End

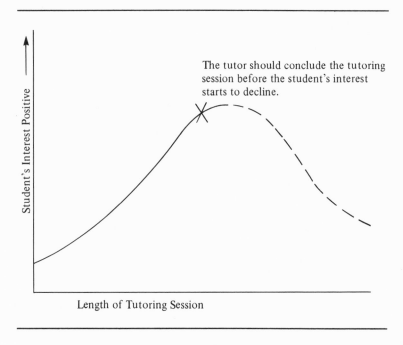

The tutor should conclude the tutoring session before the student's interest starts to decline.

Student's Interest Positive

Length of Tutoring Session

as ping pong with you, baking your student's favorite dish, etc.).

VII. Use Contingencies Carefully

In most instances, verbal praise and special recognition for achievement will be sufficient to sustain a student's motivation. However, it has been found that some students need special inducements before they will really apply themselves. If the tutor is tutoring a student whose rate of learning does not appear to represent his or her true capability, the tutor should establish appropriate contingencies to enhance the student's motivation. The use of contingencies to enhance learning is relatively simple. The tutor should identify something the student wants or enjoys and explain to him or her that if he or she achieves a particular objective by a given date, he or she will receive the contingency. For example, if an average tenth grader has established a pattern of taking twice as long to learn something as other tenth graders, the tutor may find that establishing some contingencies will help. If the student is a boy who really enjoys basketball, for example, a possible contingency would be watching the community's varsity college team work out if he learns two specific phonetic rules during the week.

One should keep the following points in mind when establishing contingencies: (1) the reward, privilege, etc., must be something that the student values; (2) the amount of time stipulated must push the student but not be unrealistic; and (3) the tutor should frequently assure the student that he or she will achieve the goal he or she is working toward if he or she applies himself or herself. Thus, he or she will receive the reward he or she is trying to earn.

VIII. Clarify Expectations

Whenever the tutor makes a request of the student, whether it is in the context of the tutoring session itself or an assignment to be completed independent of the tutoring session, the tutor should be particularly careful to specifically clarify what it is he or she wants the student to do. It has been found that the failure of many students to perform a particular task is not that they cannot perform the task, but rather that they fail to understand precisely what the expectations are. Where possible, the tutor should provide the student an example of what it is he or she wants the student to do, or how he or she wants the student to respond, whether the task is written, oral, or involves other forms of physical response. For example, if the tutor were to give the student the assignment to memorize three particular formulas, it would not be enough to merely tell the student to memorize the formulas. The tutor would also want to explain whether his or her intent was to have the student repeat the formulas orally or to write out the formulas. In addition, the tutor should clearly describe to the student any other unique stipulations related to the task.

IX. Provide the Answer for the Student if Necessary

If the student is unable to respond, or if the student responds incorrectly, the tutor should immediately provide the correct answer for the student. The tutor should not give the student hints to help him or her respond correctly; rather, the tutor should merely tell the student the correct answer and explain why it is correct. For instance, if the tutor were having the student solve a particular type of problem and the student began to apply the wrong procedures for solving it, the tutor should intervene immediately. Rather than have the student work on the problem over a period of time, when it is obvious that he or she is unable to work it correctly, the tutor should show the student how to solve the problem.

X. Points to Remember when Tutoring

The tutor should keep the following points in mind when working with a student:

1. Some students require a great deal of drill and practice with any new task.

2. Students have a great deal of tolerance for practice exercises if they are having success.

3. Students may know something one day and then forget it another.

4. Students need to overlearn some things. For example, if a student is expected to apply a particular formula in a chemistry class, it is not enough to merely apply the formula to solve one or two problems. In order to ensure that the student will, in fact, master the process of applying the

formula, he or she should be given the opportunity of applying the formula numerous times before he or she is given the exam on this particular formula.

5. The attention span of a student is generally from 30-60 minutes, depending on the maturity and disposition of the individual student. Therefore, the tutor should not attempt to work with the student longer than his or her particular span will tolerate.

6. It is extremely important that a student completely master one concept or point and then be given an opportunity to practice it numerous times before a new concept is introduced.

XI. Check to See if the Student Is Learning

The main purpose of tutoring is to help a student perform a particular task independently. The idea is to provide the student with the skills he or she needs to function more effectively in a regular academic setting independent of the tutor. In other words, the student should not become dependent on an individual tutor for success. Therefore, the tutor should consistently check to see if the student is, in fact, mastering the materials that are being covered. This is accomplished by having the student attempt the required task periodically without any help or assistance from the tutor. This procedure is called a mastery check. When the tutor decides to give a mastery check to see if a student has mastered the prescribed tasks, he or she should tell the student how he or she is doing. During the mastery check, the tutor should explain why he or she will not answer any questions or give the student suggestions. The tutor should encourage the student to do the best he or she can and not to worry about it. Checking for mastery gives the tutor some idea of what kind of progress the student is making. In addition, it helps the tutor identify particular aspects of the task with which the student may still be having difficulty.

XII. Create Opportunities for Success

Independent of a pretesting situation, the tutor should never ask a student to do something that the tutor is not relatively certain the student is able to do. In other words, the tutor should provide the student fairly extensive instructions and clarification regarding any particular task before the student is asked to attempt that task. If the task involved is a fairly complex one, the tutor might even want to break the task down into subparts and provide the student with specific instructions on how to deal with one of the subparts of the task before he or she would ask the student to attempt to perform that particular task. Ideally, the tutor should create a situation where the probability of success on the part of the student is approximately 80 percent. As the tutor conscientiously applies this rule of thumb, he or she will find that the initiative and motivation of the student will be greatly enhanced.

XIII. Teach the Student to Be Goal Oriented

As the tutor begins to work with a student, he or she should help the student make specific commitments regarding:

(1) what will be accomplished as they work together (in terms of whatever the expectations are for the student in the context of a given class). This could be preparation for a midterm, reading a certain amount of chapters, etc.; and

(2) student orientation to setting specific goals regarding the assignments he or she will do independently of the tutoring session.

Basically, there are two types of goals; those related to study habits and those related to levels of academic success. It is very useful for the student to reduce goals to writing and in some instances to discuss the goal with someone other than the tutor—close acquaintance, boyfriend, girlfriend, or anyone the student has a meaningful relationship with or respect for.

The value of goal setting will be lost unless the following points are kept in mind: (1) the goals should be realistic; (2) the goals should be clarified and referred to consistently; (3) there should be an accounting with respect to realization of specific goals; and (4) the goal selection should be appropriate to the situation. In some instances, reading a certain number of pages would be an appropriate goal, whereas in other instances, the goal may be realizing a particular grade in a class. In still another situation, the goal may be spending a minimum amount of time studying for a particular exam.

XIV. Preplan

It is absolutely essential that a tutor plan very specifically what he or she anticipates covering in a particular tutoring session as well as projecting to some degree anticipated activities over a sustained period of time. This ensures that the tutoring activities have definite direction. Under no circumstances should a tutor go into a tutoring session "cold" and then attempt to determine, once meeting with the student, the material that will be covered or dealt with during that particular tutoring session. If this occurs, the time will be generally ill-spent.

Three types of preplanning are necessary: (1) the first type deals with the material or content, concepts, etc., to be covered; (2) the second type of preparation deals with how the tutor will go about teaching the particular content; and (3) the third type deals with the assignments that are given to the student at the conclusion of the tutoring session. For example, if the prime intent of the tutor is to assess the student's mastery of basic math skills, the tutor should work out very carefully the particulars of the assessment prior to meeting with the student.

Unless a student is willing to agree to certain basic

stipulations, there is virtually no point in attempting to tutor the student. The student must agree to make an exerted effort to help himself or herself before any effort should be made to provide him or her a tutor.

In situations where a formal tutoring program exists, a basic tutor-student contract may be used. Even when this type of contract is provided, a tutor and student should still spend some time defining expectations and putting these expectations in writing.

Once the expectations are stipulated, basic decisions should be made regarding recourse if either party fails to meet the expectations that were agreed upon (loss of tutoring service, loss of opportunity to tutor, bringing such a fact to the attention of a designated person, etc.).

Procedures and Tutoring Techniques: Material Specific

In addition to the general procedures and tutoring techniques, the tutor must also be trained in procedures and techniques which are determined by the nature of the instructional materials. For example, the skills which would be requisite for a tutor in using a mathematics text would differ significantly from those skills which would be requisite for a tutor interacting with a creative writing text. Generally speaking, the more structured the instructional materials, including the specificity of the dialogue which is actually used by the tutor, the less "material specific" training is required of the tutor.

Procedures and Tutoring Techniques: Task Specific

The varied nature of instructional objectives in general necessitates the unique skills which must be transmitted to tutors. For example, the training that tutors receive for teaching students to blend sounds together is significantly different from the training that is necessary for teaching students to learn the sounds or to read simple reading exercises. In like manner, the teaching of math facts requires training which differs greatly from training directed at teaching complex division or the solution of word problems. So, not only does the training of tutors differ according to general subject areas, but training also differs according to specific instructional tasks within each subject area.

As is the case with material specific procedures, highly structured materials will most generally reduce the amount of task specific training. Conversely, relatively unstructured materials will increase the amount of specific training needed by tutors.

Since the nature and amount of specific training needed by tutors is contingent upon the degree of structure within the instructional materials, several examples of specific training will be provided in the next chapter of this book, entitled "Design Format."

Procedures and Tutoring Techniques: Record Keeping

Tutors must also be trained to keep accurate records of the student's progress. There are various reasons for always maintaining accurate records: (1) the nature and rate of the student's progress can be analyzed over time; (2) the assurance of mastery and directed review is facilitated; and (3) an alternate tutor, although not recommended, can efficiently substitute when the regular tutor is ill or for some reason can no longer tutor the student on a regular basis.

There are two types of records: (1) specific and (2) general. Specific records are designed to reflect the student's progress at specified points in the instructional sequence. Generally, specific records are needed when the instructional objectives involve several different types of learning tasks (reading, second language acquisition, etc.). The Learning Gains Summary Sheet, where pretest and posttest scores and subsequent gains are recorded, and the Record of Review Checks Passed, where mastery of review checks are recorded, are both examples of specific records which vary in design and nature according to instructional materials. Illustrations of different types of specific records and record keeping procedures will be provided in the next chapter, entitled "Design Format."

In addition to specific records and record keeping procedures are the general records and record keeping procedures. The general records include the Tutor Log, the Contingency Record, and the Progress Report.

Tutor Log. The most basic record is a record of daily tutoring activities or Tutor Log (see Figure 3). The date, the time spent in tutoring, the precise tutoring activity, and additional comments represent the data which are recorded in the Tutor Log. In addition, space should be provided to include basic information about the student (name, age, grade, school, and teacher, wherever appropriate) and the name of the tutor. A separate Tutor Log should be maintained for each student. It is essential that the tutor make a complete entry in the Tutor Log following each session. It is also important that the additional comments be as specific as possible.

Contingency Record. If the student who is being tutored is younger than 12 years of age, and if the instructional task is paired-associate in nature (learning sight words, letter names, letter sounds, math facts, etc.), the Contingency Record should be used. A separate Contingency Record should be maintained for each student under 12 years of age. The purpose of the Contingency Record is to provide a visual record of the mastery of individual stimuli. Each time mastery of an instructional prescription is demonstrated, the tutor should allow the student to place a stick star or record the date under each stimulus included in the prescription. For example, if a six-year-old is learning basic sight words, the tutor should allow the student to place a star (or draw a star if stick stars were not available) under each sight word as

Figure 3

Example of Tutor Log

Student .... Grade .... School ....
Teacher .... Tutor ....

Date	Time	Description of Activity	Comments

the student masters them (see Figure 4). If the student is ten years old, the tutor should allow the student to record the date under each sight word as it is mastered (see Figure 4). An example of a blank Contingency Record form is provided in Figure 5.

Progress Report. In addition to the Contingency Record, for students younger than 12 years of age, a Progress Report is also helpful. The purpose of the Progress Report is to provide a daily record of the student's growth for his or her parents and teachers. An example of the daily Progress Report is provided in Figure 6. The Progress Report can be nothing more than a simple note signed by the tutor.

It has been found through several years of experience that even younger tutors (10-13 years of age) can be trained to accurately maintain the Tutor Log, the Contingency Record, and the Progress Report. However, regardless of the age of the tutor, if accurate records are not maintained, maximum growth for the student cannot be guaranteed.

How to Select the Tutors

As someone starts to entertain the possibility of providing students individualized help by means of a tutor, the question immediately arises—who will do the tutoring? One thing is obvious; it must be someone who has previously mastered the objectives that are being taught. Secondly, it must be someone who is available. Interestingly enough, availability is the most difficult stipulation to meet. For example, on the surface, it would appear that a likely source of tutors for primary grade children would be high school students. However, in most instances, high school students do not prove to be a good source of tutors for primary grade children because their availability is not consistent enough. It has been found that if a primary grade child is not tutored a minimum of three times per week, the effectiveness of the tutoring is almost completely lost. It has been the authors'

Figure 4

Example of Maintaining a Contingency Record

For Younger Students:

are	there	when	to	
★	★	★		

For Older Students:

are	there	when	to	
$^{10}/_2$	$^{10}/_2$	$^{10}/_2$	$^{10}/_4$	

Figure 5

Example of a Blank Contingency Record Form

STUDENT .... TUTOR ....

Figure 6

Example of Daily Progress Report

INDIVIDUAL STUDENT PROGRESS REPORT

Student   Age

Grade   Teacher

Room No.   School

From (Date)   To (Date)

Demonstrated mastery of the following instructional prescriptions:

Tutor

INDIVIDUAL STUDENT PROGRESS REPORT

Student   Age

Grade   Teacher

Room No.   School

From (Date)   To (Date)

Demonstrated mastery of the following instructional prescriptions:

Tutor

INDIVIDUAL STUDENT PROGRESS REPORT

Student   Age

Grade   Teacher

Room No.   School

From (Date)   To (Date)

Demonstrated mastery of the following instructional prescriptions:

Tutor

experience that "in-house" tutors (students in the same building) or aides or volunteer parents are the best source of tutors. In the case of primary grade children, for example, aides, volunteer parents, or older elementary students represent the best source of tutors.

Other critical questions that arise deal primarily with supervision and training. The following are some of the authors' basic findings regarding supervision and training: (1) If students between the ages of ten and 15 are being used as tutors, they must work under the supervision of an adult. This adult must have specific expertise in devising diagnostic criterion-referenced pretests, administering pretests, preparing and maintaining adequate record sheets, preparing and organizing instructional materials, selecting student tutors, training student tutors in the use of general psychological principles of learning and specific tutoring techniques and procedures commensurate with the particular instructional objectives, making instructional prescriptions, scheduling student tutors, performing mastery checks, and devising systematic schedules for the review of instructional prescriptions previously mastered. This adult should be someone other than a classroom teacher (aide, remedial reading teacher). (2) If students 16 years of age or older or other adults are being used as tutors, they must be trained to do the following: (a) select appropriate instructional objectives; (b) devise valid pretesting procedures; (c) prepare appropriate instructional materials; (d) use established psychological principles of learning commensurate with the specific objectives; (e) maintain adequate records of rate of learning, etc.; (f) systematically check for mastery; and (g) systematically review objectives the learner has mastered previously.

In summary, the following stipulations must be met in order to ensure a high probability that students will benefit from tutoring: (1) the instructional needs of students must be diagnosed very specifically; (2) those doing the tutoring must use instructional materials commensurate with specific instructional needs of a student; (3) those doing the tutoring must be trained in the use of established psychological principles of learning and validated objectives; (4) records must be maintained that report the following: the performance of individual students on specific pretests; a description of each instructional prescription and the date it was made; the date the student achieved mastery of each instructional prescription; the dates when instructional prescriptions previously mastered were reviewed; the performance of individual students on specific criterion tests and the date the tests were administered; (5) if those doing the tutoring are under 15 years of age, they must work under the supervision of an adult who has specific expertise; and (6) if those doing the tutoring are 15 years of age or older, they must be trained to do specific things with precision. These basic stipulations constitute Structured Tutoring and are the stipulations that are not complied with by practitioners of most tutorial projects.

The effective use of human resources as tutors (peers, secondary students, teacher aides, volunteer parents, etc.) is to this date a virtually untapped source of manpower available to the public schools as well as other centers of education. At the present time, teacher-training colleges provide prospective teachers training in methodology and use of materials and media, but they do not provide prospective teachers expertise in how to make effective use of human resources. Consequently, teachers are generally at a loss regarding how parents, aides, etc., may be involved in the instructional process. If teacher-training colleges would provide teachers expertise in how to train and manage human resources, based on the Structured Tutoring model, their potential effectiveness would be enhanced significantly.

Summary

The name Structured Tutoring implies a tutoring model characterized by a very precise tutor-student relationship and highly structured instructional materials. Research has repeatedly demonstrated that the tutoring relationship and the instructional materials are relatively complex components which cannot be left to chance. Training techniques and procedures for Structured Tutoring fall into four categories: (1) general, (2) material specific, (3) task specific, and (4) record keeping. The general techniques and procedures as well as general aspects of record keeping apply to all tutoring relationships and are not determined by the desired instructional objectives or the nature of the instructional materials. Specific techniques and procedures, on the other hand, are governed by the instructional objectives and materials. In addition to meeting these four criteria, selection of tutors is based upon: (1) the tutors having previously mastered the objectives being taught, and (2) the availability and consistency of tutors. It is clear that Structured Tutoring systems are more rigorous than most existing tutoring programs. While the goals may be similar in other tutoring processes, the focus on methods in Structured Tutoring is more specific, as characterized by the four sets of concerns addressed in this chapter. For this reason, the authors contend that Structured Tutoring is indeed effective, while tutoring in general is not.

The effective use of human resources to date is a virtually untapped source of manpower available to the public schools as well as other centers of education. It is the authors' position that the Structured Tutoring model is the key to the effective use of human resources (parents, aides, volunteers, and students) because the Structured Tutoring approach helps ensure that nonprofessionals will be effective when they work with individual students. Training in the management of human resources should either be an integral part of teacher-training programs or an area specialization at the graduate level. Unless this happens on a large scale, the effective use of human resources in the instructional process will not be realized and, therefore, the individual needs of many students will not be met.

References

Harrison, G.V. Training Students to Tutor. Technical Memorandum 2686/000/00. Santa Monica, California: System Development Corporation, September 28, 1967.

Niedermeyer, F.C. The Effects of Training on the Instructional Behaviors of Student Tutors. Southwest Regional Laboratory Research Memorandum, March 30, 1969.

III.

DESIGN FORMAT

In the previous chapter, a concise description of the nature of the tutoring relationship was provided. In particular, the general tutoring techniques and procedures as well as general record keeping procedures were discussed. However, it was stated that specific techniques and procedures (material specific and task specific) as well as certain record keeping procedures are determined to a great extent by the nature of the instructional objectives being transferred to the student. The objectives of this chapter are (1) to provide a more detailed look at the nature of the instructional design itself (as it is determined by the desired instructional objectives); and (2) to provide examples of specific techniques and procedures, including examples of specific records and record keeping procedures.

Types of Learning

Since the specific training a tutor should receive is dependent upon the type of instructional outcomes the tutor will be teaching, it is necessary to look at a general classification of instructional objectives. Most desired instructional outcomes which warrant a one-to-one tutorial experience can usually be categorized under one of the following five classifications:

    1. Stimulus-Response Learning (such as naming the basic digits).

2. Computation (such as addition and subtraction).
3. Application of Specific Rules (such as when to drop the letter "y" and add "-ies").
4. Performance (such as a science experiment or shooting a basketball).
5. Reading. Because the process of reading is so complex, it must be classified under a separate heading even though some aspects of reading involve stimulus-response learning and the application of specific rules.

To help the reader understand the following discussion of the five steps of Structured Tutoring, examples will deal only with stimulus-response tasks which are common to everyone. Examples which deal with content that might be uncommon to the reader will be intentionally omitted.

Five Steps of Structured Tutoring

There are five basic steps associated with the Structured Tutoring model:

Step 1: Preassess the student's present ability.
Step 2: Prepare to tutor the student.
Step 3: Tutor the student using the proper tutoring techniques and procedures.
Step 4: Maintain the appropriate records.
Step 5: Review the student's progress.

Each of these steps will be discussed in detail in the pages that follow.

Step 1: Preassess the Student's Present Ability

1A. Select Appropriate Instructional Outcomes

Many tutors fail to help students overcome learning difficulties because they do not identify instructional outcomes that are specific enough. In order to be effective, the tutor must take steps to identify as precisely as possible what he or she is going to help the student to learn. Unless this is done, most of the time the tutor spends on an individual basis with the student will be wasted. For example, if the tutor sets as his or her desired instructional outcome, "improving the student's reading ability," it is not likely that he or she will be successful in helping the student; the outcome is too broad. However, if the tutor finds the student unable to produce the sounds of most consonants and sets as the desired instructional outcome, "the student will be able to produce without hesitation the sounds of every consonant," he or she will have a better chance of helping the student.

Consider What the Student Needs to Know

Figures 7A-7D list examples of instructional outcomes involving stimulus-response learning for students of varying ages. The instructional outcomes suggested in Figures 7A-7D will, therefore, prove to be appropriate for many students. The process of selecting an instructional outcome for a particular student should involve several factors:

1. The most important factor in selecting an instructional outcome is to determine what the student is currently expected to know. For the most part, students are expected to learn predetermined skills in designated grades. For this reason, if a student has not mastered what he or she is expected to know at a given grade level, he or she will fall farther and farther behind. Such deficiencies should therefore receive first priority when selecting a desired instructional outcome for a student.

2. A second major consideration in selecting instructional outcomes is to determine what the student will encounter in the near future in the regular classroom. For example, if certain sounds are going to be covered soon by the student's second grade teacher, these particular sounds would make excellent instructional outcomes, especially for the student who is slower to learn through classroom instruction.

Learning these sounds would prepare him or her for what is to come and give him or her a chance for success.

3. Another major consideration in selecting instructional outcomes is to determine in what areas the student shows an interest. For example, if a young child shows an interest in numbers, the tutor might select naming the numbers as an instructional outcome. Or, if an older student is interested in political science, the tutor might select identifying platforms of political parties as the outcome.

4. The last consideration in selecting an instructional outcome is to carefully weigh the classroom teacher's judgment. The tutor should ask the student's teacher to go through the instructional outcomes suggested in Figures 7A-7D and select those with which he or she feels the student needs help.

If the teacher or tutor selects desired instructional outcomes other than those types which are represented in Figures 7A-7D, he or she should make certain that the instructional outcomes he or she selects require the student to make a designated response to a single stimulus that does not require computation skills or application of rules. Again, the procedures specified in this chapter apply *only* to instructional outcomes that require the student to respond to specified stimuli based on straight recall.

For example, Johnny, a sixth-grade student, is evidencing difficulty with classroom instruction in English. In conversing with Johnny's teacher, the tutor finds that all sixth-grade students should learn to read a list of 200 basic vocabulary words as part of the general English requirement. The tutor notes by referring to Figure 7B that learning to pronounce words is an example of stimulus-response learning, and so it is decided that Johnny should receive tutorial instruction based on the techniques and procedures in this book. Once Johnny learns to read the words, the tutor might want to help Johnny learn the meaning of each word that he doesn't

Figure 7A

Examples of Stimulus-Response Instructional Outcomes

Pre-School

The child will name the lower/upper case letters of the alphabet without hesitation and when they are presented out of order.

The child will name the digits 1-20 without hesitation and when they are presented out of order.

The child will name basic geometric shapes (e.g., △, □,○, etc.) without hesitation.

The child will name the eight basic colors (red, yellow, blue, orange, green, purple, white, black) without hesitation.

The child will name without hesitation common objects or animals that were previously unknown by the child (e.g., orange, tiger, etc.).

Figure 7B

Examples of Stimulus-Response Instructional Outcomes

Primary Grades

The child will produce the sounds of the consonants without hesitation.

The child will produce the short sound of all five vowels without hesitation.

The child will produce the sounds of the common digraphs and blends without hesitation (e.g., th, sh, wh, fl, bl, pr, etc.).

The child will read 200 basic sight words without hesitation (e.g., the, they, said, go, for, because, etc.).

The child will name designated historical characters without hesitation when presented with their pictures (e.g., George Washington, Benjamin Franklin, Abraham Lincoln, etc.).

The child will orally provide synonyms for 500 basic words without hesitation (e.g., glad, funny, pretty, bad, hot, etc.).

The child will name the digits 20-100 without hesitation when they are presented out of order.

The child will read three-digit numbers without hesitation (e.g., 137, 546, 389, etc.).

The child will say the time of day without hesitation when presented with pictures of clocks either at the hour or half past the hour.

The child will say without hesitation the names of the months of the year when presented with abbreviations of the names.

The child will name the basic signs without hesitation (e.g., +, -, x, %, ¢, etc.).

Figure 7C

Examples of Stimulus-Response Instructional Outcomes

Upper Elementary Grades

The student will name without hesitation each of the 50 states when shown its geometric outline.

The student will be able to recall without hesitation 20 basic facts that the student's teacher feels the student should know (e.g.: How many feet are in a mile?, What's the capital of California?, etc.).

The student will read four-digit numbers without hesitation (e.g., 1,755, 1,230, 9,672, etc.).

The student will state without hesitation the number of sides corresponding to specified polygons: hexagon, decagon, dodecagon, triangle.

The student will state without hesitation the following metric units in terms of meters or fractions of a meter: hectometer, decameter, decimeter, centimeter, kilometer, millimeter.

The student will give without hesitation the English equivalent of the following Spanish words: coche, libro, casa, iglesia, boca, ojos.

The student will be able to read 20 new vocabulary words without hesitation (e.g., quatrain, converge, prohibit, etc.).

The student will be able to convert to decimal notation without hesitation the following fractions: 1/4, 1/2, 1/3, 1/5, 1/8, 1/10.

The student will orally provide the definitions of the following prefixes without hesitation: re-, ab-, ad-, be-, com-, en-, de-, pro-.

Figure 7D

Examples of Stimulus-Response Instructional Outcomes

Secondary Grades

The student will identify without hesitation the following standard abbreviations which have been adopted for describing lumber: S4S, K.D., Quar., S2S.

The student will identify without hesitation the names of the chemical solutions which correspond to the following symbols: HCl, NaCl, CH_3OH, KBr, BaC_{12}.

The student will correctly define without hesitation the following fields of science: chemistry, astronomy, meteorology, botany, geology, biology.

The student will identify without hesitation the color which identifies the following chemicals when heated: sodium, potassium, tungsten, chromium, mercury.

The student will identify without hesitation the phylum to which each of the following belong: robin, starfish, tapeworm, rose, spider, seaweed.

The student will identify without hesitation the specific vitamin deficiency which causes the following disorders: pellagra, scurvy, rickets, cataracts, beriberi.

The student will identify without hesitation the type of joint associated with the following parts of the human skeletal system: shoulder, elbow, knee, spinal column, cranium, hip.

The student will state without hesitation all of the elements of the Periodic Chart, given the symbol for each element.

The student will identify without hesitation the basic joints used in gas and arc welding.

The student will identify without hesitation the parts of the ear when given a diagram of the ear.

---

know. Since this objective is more complex than simple stimulus-response learning, the tutor would need to refer to the procedures for teaching the meaning of vocabulary words found in the Structured Tutoring reading materials. (See the chapter of this book entitled "Resources.")

State Outcomes in Writing

Once the appropriate instructional outcomes are selected for a particular student, it is advantageous to state in writing the behavior that will be accepted on the part of the student as evidence that he or she has achieved each instructional outcome. The following guidelines will assist the tutor in preparing such a written statement:

1. The instructional outcome should be stated in terms of student performance, *not* teaching activity.

CORRECT: The student will be able to read without hesitation each of the basic 200 vocabulary words.

INCORRECT: I will teach the student to read each of the basic 200 vocabulary words without hesitation.

2. Because of the nature of stimulus-response learning, it is very important to stipulate that the student will provide the desired response (correct answer) without hesitation.

CORRECT: The student will be able to read without hesitation each of the basic 200 vocabulary words.

INCORRECT: The student will be able to read each of the basic 200 vocabulary words.

3. If there is any sequence associated with a particular collection of stimuli (such as naming digits or letters of the alphabet), the statement should stipulate that the student will be able to provide the desired response for each stimulus when the stimuli are presented out of sequence.

CORRECT: The student will be able to produce the

correct sound for each consonant in the alphabet (within one second) when it is presented randomly.

INCORRECT: The student will be able to produce the correct sound for each consonant in the alphabet.

In many instances, a student will eventually need to learn to produce a series of stimuli sequentially (such as naming digits or letters of the alphabet). Initially, however, a student should be able to respond correctly to this type of stimuli independent of a sequence.

1B. Pretest the Student

Once a specific instructional outcome is selected for a student, it is very important that a valid measure be constructed for the purpose of determining the student's ability to deal with the particular group of stimuli that have been selected. This is accomplished by giving the student a pretest consisting of the group of stimuli included in the desired instructional outcome. In some instances, the instructional outcomes may consist of several different groups or collections of stimuli. If this is the case, separate pretests should be constructed for each group or collection of stimuli. The tutor should be careful to adhere to the following procedures when he or she constructs and administers a pretest.

What to Include in the Pretest

Each pretest should include the following:

- A place for the student's name.
- A place to record the date the pretest was administered.
- A place to record the age and grade of the student.
- A place to record the name of the person who administered the pretest.

- A place to record the name or the school the student attends.
- A place for each of the stimuli specified in a particular instructional outcome. Care should be taken to ensure that the style of letters (numbers, format, etc.) used on the pretest is commensurate with the style used in the school. If the stimuli are symbols and the student being tested is a primary-grade child, one should make certain that the stimuli on the pretest are slightly larger than normal type. The stimuli should be spaced evenly on the pretest (at least one-half inch between stimuli). *Note:* If the group of stimuli has a sequence associated with them (such as *a, b, c, d,* or 1, 2, 3, 4, 5), make certain that they are *not* in sequence on the pretest (use an order such as *b, c, a, d,* or 5, 3, 2, 1, 4).
- Specific instructions that will be read to the student. These instructions should include: (1) an explanation so that the student will know how he or she should respond; (2) an explanation as to what the student should say if he or she does not know an answer; (3) a statement designed to ensure that the student will not become anxious if there are several answers he or she does not know; and (4) one example. Figure 8 depicts a portion of the 200-word pretest that would be used in our example with Johnny, a sixth-grade student.

The instructional outcome that the pretest in Figure 8 is designed to test is: The student will read the following vocabulary words without hesitation: *obstruct, prey, progenitor, prohibit, converge, hexagon, ascend, quatrain, denizen, solemn, reflex, democracy.*

What Procedures to Follow During the Pretest

These procedures should be followed when a student is pretested:

Figure 8

Sample Pretest

Student's Name .... Age ....

Grade .... School .... Date ....

Examiner ....

Directions: "When I point to a word, you read the word. For example, if I pointed to this word (point to *quatrain*), you would say 'quatrain.' If you do not know a word, say 'I don't know it.' Do not worry if there are words you do not know."

obstruct	prohibit	ascend	solemn
prey	converge	quatrain	reflex
progenitor	hexagon	denizen	democracy

- Before administering the test, ask the student two or three simple questions about pets, hobbies, or special interests.
- Make it a point to speak in a friendly voice while you are testing the student.
- Read the directions to the student.
- Point to the stimulus with the end of your pencil when you want the student to respond to the stimulus.
- Do *not* tell the student if his or her response is correct.
- If the student hesitates longer than one second, mark the response as incorrect (such as (prey)), and say something like this: "Don't worry if you don't know

it. Let's try the next one." Then go to the next stimulus.

- If the student's response is correct, circle the stimulus (such as (prey)).
- If the student's response is incorrect, if the student hesitates longer than one second before responding correctly, or if the student is unable to respond, this mark ((⊘)) goes around the stimulus (such as (prey)). *Note:* The reason for marking both the correct and incorrect responses is so that the student will not know which items the tutor is marking incorrect. This is particularly important for younger children.
- Praise the student generally at the conclusion of the test.
- *After the student is excused,* go back and put a slash through each incorrect response (see Figure 9). This is done so that someone other than the tutor can interpret the test results by referring to the test itself.
- If the student being tested is six years of age or younger, he or she should not be required to respond to more than 30 stimuli in a pretesting session. Therefore, if the desired instructional outcome selected involves more than 30 stimuli, the pretest should be administered in two or more sessions. If the student being tested is seven years of age or older, he or she should not be required to respond to more than 100 stimuli in a pretesting session. For example, to test Johnny's ability to read the 200 basic vocabulary words, at least two pretests would be constructed of no more than 100 vocabulary words each.

Figure 9

Example of Marking Each Incorrect Response

SAMPLE PRETEST

Student's Name *Johnny Sanderson* Age *13*

Grade *sixth* School *Limerick* Date *6/15/77*

Examiner *C. Dixon*

Directions: "When I point to a word, you read the word. For example, if I pointed to this word (point to *quatrain*), you would say 'quatrain.' If you do not know a word, say 'I don't know it.' Do not worry if there are words you do not know."

obstruct	pro~~h~~ibit	ascend	so~~l~~emn
p~~r~~ey	con~~v~~erge	qua~~t~~rain	reflex
pro~~g~~enitor	he~~x~~agon	de~~n~~izen	democracy

Note: After the pretest is completed and the student is excused, go back and put a slash through each incorrect response.

1C. Record the Student's Performance on a Profile Sheet

A Profile Sheet should be designed to report the following information at a glance:

- A brief description of the task.
- The stimuli specified in the desired instructional outcome.
- The date the pretest was administered.

- The student's performance on the pretest.
- The date the tutor begins to teach each particular stimulus (prescription date).
- The date when the student is able to respond correctly to each particular stimulus (mastery date).
- The ability of the student to respond correctly to stimuli at a later date (review check).
- The ability of the student to respond correctly to every stimulus that was on the pretest at a later date after the student has been tutored (posttest).

Figure 10 provides an illustration of a portion of the Profile Sheet based on Johnny's performance. The first thing that is recorded on this Profile Sheet is a brief description of the task specified in the instructional outcome. This is written to the right of "Task" (see Figure 11). The second thing that is recorded on the Profile Sheet is each stimulus included in the pretest. The stimuli are recorded in the boxes to the right of "Stimuli" (see Figure 12). If the instructional outcomes involve more than one group or collection of stimuli, separate Profile Sheets should be maintained for each group or collection.

After you pretest a student, record the student's performance on the Profile Sheet. This is done by recording the date the pretest was administered and putting a plus (+) under each stimulus the student responded to correctly on the pretest and a zero (0) under each stimulus the student was unable to respond to correctly (see Figure 13). (Instructions on how other information is recorded on the Profile Sheet will be discussed at a later point in this chapter.)

If the tutor decides to deal with several different groups or collections of stimuli, he or she may need more than one Profile Sheet for the student. For instance, in our example where the tutor wishes to teach Johnny to read 200 vocabulary words, several Profile Sheets will be needed. In addition, if the tutor is working with more than one student,

Figure 10

Portion of Profile Sheet Based on Student's Performance

PROFILE SHEET

Student *Johnny Sanderson*. Age .....*13*...... Grade ..*sixth*........

Task *Reading Basic Vocabulary Words*

Stimuli	abstruct	prey	progenitor	prohibit	converse	hexagon	ascend	quatrain
Pretest Date **6/15/77**	+	O	O	O	O	O	+	O.
Prescription Date		6/17/77	6/17/77	6/17/77	6/17/77	6/17/77		6/17/77
Mastery Date		6/20/77	6/20/77	6/20/77	6/20/77	6/20/77		6/20/77
Review Check	7/8 +	7/8 +	7/8 +	7/8 +	7/8 +	7/8 +	7/8 +	7/8 +
Review Check	9/25 +	9/25 +	9/25 +	9/25 +	9/25 +	9/25 +	9/25 +	9/25 +
Posttest Date **10/20/77**	+	+	+	+	+	+	+	+

Figure 11

Example of Recording Task in Profile Sheet

Student *Johnny Sanderson*. Age ...*13*... Grade ..*sixth*........
Task   *Reading Basic Vocabulary Words*

Stimuli							

Figure 12

Example of Stimuli on Profile Sheet

Student *Johnny Sanderson*.. Age ..*13*.... Grade *sixth*..........
Task   *Reading Basic Vocabulary Words*

Stimuli	*obstruct*	*prey*	*progenitor*	*prohibit*	*converge*	*hexagon*	*ascend*
Pretest Date							

Figure 13

Example of Pretest Performance on Profile Sheet

Student *Johnny Sanderson*.. Age ...*13*.. Grade ..*sixth*........
Task   *Reading Basic Vocabulary Words*

Stimuli	*obstruct*	*prey*	*progenitor*	*prohibit*	*converge*	*hexagon*	*ascend*
Pretest Date *6/15/77*	+	o	o	o	o	o	+

a separate Profile Sheet should be maintained for each student.

An example of a blank Profile Sheet is provided in Figure 14.

Step 2: Prepare to Tutor the Student

2A. Prepare Instructional Materials

The tutor should prepare a set of 3" by 5" flash cards. Three flash cards are needed for *each* stimulus the student missed on the pretest. For example, if the desired instructional outcome is, "the student will name without hesitation the lower case letters of the alphabet when presented them in random order," the tutor would prepare three flash cards for each letter of the alphabet the student was unable to identify correctly without hesitation on the pretest. If the instructional outcome is, "the student will name without hesitation each element when presented with its symbol in random order," the tutor would prepare three flash cards with the symbol for each element the student was unable to identify without hesitation on the pretest. If heavier paper is used in preparing the flash cards, they will be much easier to handle.

Every effort should be made to use the style of writing used by the student's elementary or secondary school and to make the stimulus identical on the three flash cards.

Once the flash cards are prepared, the upper-right corner of the cards should be clipped so that there will not be any difficulty in keeping the flash cards right side up when the tutor works with the student (see Figure 15).

The flash cards should be kept in a file box or packet. In addition, index cards should be used to organize the flash cards (see Figure 16).

2B. Prepare a Tutor Log

Before the tutor begins to work with the student, the tutor

Figure 14

Example of a Blank Profile Sheet

Student .... Age .... Grade .... Teacher .... Room ....

Task

Stimuli													
Pretest Date													
Prescription Date													
Mastery Date													
Review Check													
Review Check													
Posttest Date													

Stimuli													
Pretest Date													
Prescription Date													
Mastery Date													
Review Check													
Review Check													
Posttest Date													

Figure 15

Example of Flash Cards

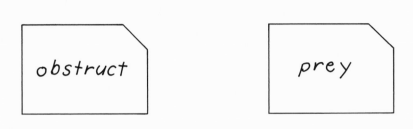

Figure 16

Example of Flash Cards File Box

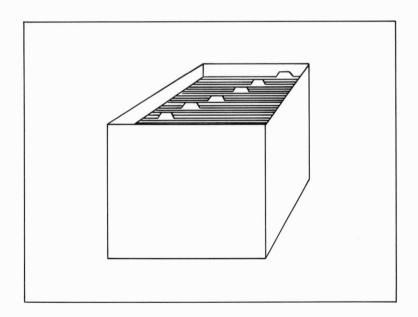

should prepare a Tutor Log. The procedures for designing and maintaining a Tutor Log are found in the preceding chapter of this book. If the tutor is working with more than one student, a separate Tutor Log should be maintained for each student.

2C. Specify Instructional Prescriptions

It has been found that if too many new stimuli are introduced at one time, a student will have difficulty learning the answers for the stimuli. In contrast, if a limited number of new stimuli are introduced at one time, and if subsequent groups of about the same number of new stimuli are introduced as each previous group is mastered, the student will learn the new stimuli more quickly.

In order to facilitate the student's mastery of the stimuli missed on the pretest, the tutor should divide the total number of stimuli missed on the pretest into specific instructional prescriptions. An instructional prescription consists of approximately five stimuli. For example, if the tutor intended to teach a student 20 stimuli (those stimuli the student missed on the pretest), he or she would divide the total group into four instructional prescription groups of five stimuli each. In other words, if the student was unable to produce the sounds of the letters c, d, g, f, j, h, l, k, m, p, n, r, u, s, w, v, y, t, z, and x when pretested, the instructional prescriptions should be designated as follows:

Instructional Prescription 1: c, d, g, f, j
Instructional Prescription 2: h, l, k, m, p
Instructional Prescription 3: n, r, u, s, w
Instructional Prescription 4: v, y, t, z, x

When the tutor works with the student, he or she should only work with those stimuli specified in the instructional prescription. He or she should not focus on every stimulus the student missed on the pretest at one time. The number of stimuli included in an instructional prescription is dependent

many more stimuli than they would otherwise be able to learn.

Before a tutor attempts to work with a student, he or she should review these specific tutoring techniques and procedures very carefully and then practice the flash card drills with someone other than the student to be tutored. Then, once the tutor has practiced using these drills, he or she should carefully reread this section and the general techniques and procedures in the preceding chapter before attempting to tutor a student. It is absolutely essential that the tutor have both the general and the specific techniques well in mind before he or she begins to tutor. In addition, the tutor should review these two chapters every week or so until he or she is totally conversant with them. The effectiveness of a tutor depends almost exclusively on how closely the tutor follows the general and specific techniques and procedures discussed in these two chapters.

The following three flash card steps should be followed each time a new instructional prescription is introduced to the student.

**FLASH CARD STEP 1: Rehearse the correct answers
with the student.**

It has been found that because of a history of repeated failure, many students become very anxious when they are asked to respond to a stimulus for which they do not know the answer. Therefore, it is extremely important that each time a new instructional prescription is introduced, the correct responses (answers) are rehearsed with the student before the student is asked to answer independently.

To rehearse the correct answers with the student, the following procedures should be used:

- Place one flash card for each stimulus in the specific instructional prescription in a stack.
- Present the flash cards one at a time, tell the student the correct answer, and have him or her repeat it.
  (Example: Hold up a flash card with the word "quatrain" on it.)
    Tutor: "Quatrain"
    Student: "Quatrain"
    Tutor: "Very good."

- Each time the student repeats the answer correctly, praise him or her by saying "That is right" or "Very good." It is extremely important that the student is praised consistently each time he or she repeats the answer correctly.
- If the student is prone to whisper, ask him or her to repeat the answer more loudly. When the student repeats the answer more loudly, give him or her special praise.
- As the tutor first begins to rehearse the answers for a particular instructional prescription, he or she should not expose the flash cards too rapidly. However, he or she should gradually increase the rate until the student is repeating one response every two seconds. If the tutor fails to maintain this rate of exposure, the student will lose interest.
- In some instances, the tutor may not want to do anything more than simply rehearse the correct answers the first time he or she works with the student. The tutor should not, under any circumstances, go on to FLASH CARD STEP 2 until he or she is certain the student can correctly respond to some of the cards before being told the correct answer.
- As mentioned previously, at the conclusion of each tutoring session, an entry should be made in the Tutor Log (see Figure 18).

FLASH CARD STEP 2: Check for learning.
- Place one flash card in the stack for the group of stimuli the tutor has been rehearsing with the student.
- Say: "Okay, now let's see if you can tell me the answers without my helping you."
- Say: "When I hold up a flash card, you tell me the correct answer if you can. If you do not know the answer, say, 'I don't know.' "
- Do *not* tell the student the correct answers.
- Hold up one flash card at a time.
- If the student is able to answer correctly, *do not* say anything. Instead, place the flash card face up on the table in front of the student and go on to the next flash card. If the student is slow to answer (hesitates longer than one second), the tutor should place the flash card face down in front of himself or herself and then go on to the next card. *NOTE*: Since this learning check is a form of test, the tutor should not tell the student if his or her answers are correct or incorrect.
- Praise the student's general performance.

If the student is able to answer correctly to at least two stimuli, the tutor should go on to the next step. If the student is unable to answer correctly to at least two stimuli, the tutor should continue to rehearse the correct answers with the student until he or she learns to answer correctly to at least two stimuli.

Figure 18

Example of Activities on Tutor Log

TUTOR LOG

Student *Johnny Sanderson* ... Tutor ...... *C. Dixon* ....

Date	Time	Description of Activity	Comments
⁶/₁₇/₇₇	10 min.	had Johnny rehearse the words: obstruct, prey, progenitor, prohibit, converge.	he spoke very softly and was timid
⁶/₁₉/₇₇	5 min.	rehearsed the words: obstruct, prey, progenitor, prohibit, converge.	he started to speak louder

---

The tutor should record on the Tutor Log the stimuli the student learned as a result of rehearsing the correct responses and the date he or she checked the student for learning (see Figure 19).

In some instances, students will learn to respond correctly to every stimulus in the instructional prescription from the rehearsal drill in FLASH CARD STEP 1. If this proves to be the case, the tutor does not need to use the drill specified in Step 3 for teaching the remaining new answers. He or she would simply drill the student (have the student respond to the group of stimuli without telling him or her the correct answers and consistently praise the student each time he or she responds correctly) for approximately ten minutes a day for two consecutive days and then proceed to introduce the next instructional prescription. When a new prescription is introduced, the tutor should start with the rehearsal drill in FLASH CARD STEP 1 as was done with the first prescription. *NOTE*: Once the student knows at least two of the answers in the instructional prescription, the tutor does *not* rehearse the correct answer any longer with the student. The rehearsal step is appropriate only when the tutor begins to teach the student a completely new instructional prescription.

Figure 19

Example of Rehearsing and Learning
Check on Tutor Log

Date	Time	Description of Activity	Comments
6/17/77	10 min.	had Johnny rehearse the words: obstruct, prey, progenitor, prohibit, converge.	he spoke very softly and was timid
6/19/77	5 min.	rehearsed the words: obstruct, prey, progenitor, prohibit, converge.	he started to speak louder
6/19/77	3 min.	checked the student for learning.	Johnny knew the words "obstruct" & "prohibit"

FLASH CARD STEP 3: Teach the remaining new answers.

Once the student has learned to give the correct response to at least two answers, the following procedures should be used to teach the student the rest of the answers in the instructional prescription.

Before the Tutor Meets with the Student

- Place the stimuli the student was able to answer correctly in a separate stack (such as one flash card for "obstruct" and one flash card for "prohibit").
- Combine *three* flash cards of *one* stimulus the student did not know when he or she was checked for learning (such as three flash cards for "converge") with the flash cards the student was able to answer correctly ("obstruct" and "prohibit").
- Shuffle the stack of flash cards and make certain that the cards showing the new stimulus are *not* the first in the stack. It is important that the first card in the stack be a card for which the student knows the answer (see Figure 20).

When the Tutor Meets with the Student

- The tutor should tell the student what he or she wants done: "When

Figure 20

*Examples of Flash Cards Used
to Teach Remaining New Answers*

Example #1:

Flash cards included in the stack are:

Explanation: The student was able to read the words "obstruct" and "prohibit" when checked for learning. The word "converge" is the new stimulus being introduced.

Example #2:

Flash cards included in the stack are:

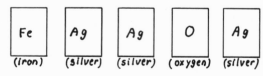

Explanation: The student was able to name iron (Fe) and oxygen (O) when checked for learning. The symbol for silver is the new stimulus being introduced.

I hold up a flash card, you tell me the correct answer if you can. This time I will not tell you the correct answer unless you need help."

- Show the student one flash card at a time.
- If the student answers correctly, say "right" or "very good" and go on to the next card.
- If the student hesitates for more than one second before answering, tell the student the correct answer and have him or her repeat the correct answer. When the student repeats the correct answer, praise the student and go on to the next card.
- If the student answers incorrectly, do *not* say, "no." Simply tell the student the correct answer and have him or her repeat it. When the student is able to repeat the correct answer, praise the student and go on to the next card.
- If the student answers correctly but speaks very softly, praise him or her and then suggest that he or she speak more loudly. Once the student repeats the answer more loudly, extend special praise by saying "That was particularly good" and then go on to the next card.
- When the student starts to answer correctly to the stimulus the tutor is teaching, he or she should be given special praise. The tutor should say things like "Very good, you really learned that one in a hurry" or "Right, you are really doing well!"
- It is very important that the tutor speaks up when he or she praises the student. The effectiveness of verbal praise is lost if the tutor is prone to mumble when he or she tells the student his or her answer is right.
- When the tutor starts to teach the student a new answer, he or she should not expose the flash cards too fast at first, but gradually increase the rate until the student is responding to one flash card per second. If the tutor fails to maintain this rate of exposure, the student will lose interest.
- Once the student is able to respond correctly each time the new stimulus comes up, the tutor should continue to drill the student for about five minutes.
- Once the student is able to give consistent and correct answers each time the first new stimulus comes up over a period of approximately five minutes, the tutor should then follow the procedures specified below to teach the second new answer:
  1. Remove one of the three flash cards for the answer just learned from the stack (such as "converge" or "Ag" [silver]).
  2. Add three flash cards for the second answer the student did not know during the Learning Check in FLASH CARD STEP 2.
  3. Follow the same drill procedure as was used to teach the first new answer (see Figure 21).

Figure 21

*Examples of Flash Cards Used to Teach
Second New Answer*

Example #1:

Flash cards included in the stack are:

obstruct	prey	converge	prey	converge	prey	prohibit

Explanation: The student has learned the words "obstruct" and "prohibit" from rehearsing the answers in the rehearsal step. The first new answer introduced after the Learning Check step is "converge," and the second new answer that is now being introduced is "prey."

Example #2:

Flash cards included in the stack are:

Fe	U	Ag	U	Ag	U	O
(iron)	(uranium)	(silver)	(uranium)	(silver)	(uranium)	(oxygen)

Explanation: The student has learned Fe (iron) and O (oxygen) from rehearsing the answers; Ag (silver) was the first new answer introduced and U (uranium) is the second new answer being introduced.

- Once the student is able to give consistent and correct answers each time the second new answer comes up over a period of approximately five minutes, the tutor should follow the procedures specified below to teach the third new answer:
  1. Remove one more flash card for the first new answer taught (such as "converge" or "Ag" [silver]).
  2. Remove one of the three flash cards for the second answer taught (such as "prey" or "U" [uranium]).
  3. Add three flash cards for the third new answer (such as "progenitor").
  4. Follow the same drill procedure as was used to teach the first new answer (see Figure 22).
- If there are additional new answers in the instructional prescription, continue to retain one flash card for each answer the student knew before the last new answer was introduced, two flash cards for the last new answer introduced, and three flash cards for the new answer being introduced.
- It is important to note that with younger students (five or six years of age) the tutor should only introduce *one* new answer each time he or she works with the student. If the student is seven years of age or older, the tutor can introduce two new answers each time he or she works with the student. However, if the student consistently has trouble answering correctly for one or more of the stimuli introduced in previous sessions, the tutor should *not* introduce any new stimuli until the student is able to answer correctly on two successive sessions for each flash card.
- Do not assume a student has mastered an instructional prescription when the student is able to respond to each stimulus in the prescription immediately following a drill. The tutor may assume that the student has mastered the prescription when the student can respond correctly to each stimulus a minimum of one consecutive day following the drill.
- When a prescription is mastered, the tutor should introduce the next instructional prescription. When a new prescription is introduced, the tutor should place one flash card for each stimulus of the new prescription in a stack. Then he or she should begin by having the student rehearse the correct answers as described in FLASH CARD STEP 1. He or she should then follow the same procedures that were used to teach the first instructional prescription. The tutor should not retain in the stack any of the flash cards from the previous prescription.

Figure 22

Example of Flash Cards Used to Teach
Third New Answer

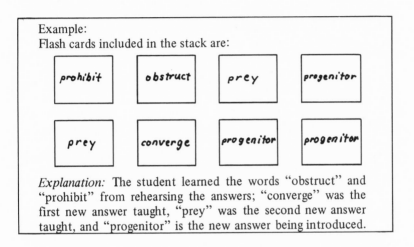

Example:
Flash cards included in the stack are:

Explanation: The student learned the words "obstruct" and "prohibit" from rehearsing the answers; "converge" was the first new answer taught, "prey" was the second new answer taught, and "progenitor" is the new answer being introduced.

When the Tutor Concludes a Tutoring Session

At the conclusion of each tutoring session, the tutor should praise the student's general performance and then summarize what the student has learned. This is done by making appropriate entries in the Tutor Log and the Profile Sheet. In addition, if the student is younger than 12 years of age, the tutor should have the student make an entry in the Contingency Record and give the student a note in the form of a Progress Report to take to his or her parents and teachers (see Figure 23).

It is important that the tutor explain very carefully why he or she is writing the note. If the tutor does not clarify the purpose of the note or Progress Report, the student may become fearful. Unfortunately, most notes that go home deal

Figure 23

Example of a Progress Report

> *Tutor:*   "Because you did so well today, I am going
> to write a note to your mother and tell her
> how well you did."
>
> > *Johnny did very well today.*
> > *He learned to read the words*
> > *"obstruct" and "prohibit."*
> >   *Claudia Dixon*
> > *student tutor*

---

with misbehavior rather than with accomplishment on the
part of the student. Once the note is written, the tutor
should read it to the student. With older students, writing a
note may not be appropriate. In general, verbal praise is more
effective with older students.

At the conclusion of the session, the student should also
be told when his or her next session will be with the tutor.

Step 4: Maintain the Appropriate Records

4A. Maintain a Record of the Student's Progress

When a student can respond correctly on two consecutive
days for each stimulus in a particular instructional prescription, the date is recorded under each stimulus in the

"Mastery Date" column of the Profile Sheet (see Figure 24A).

The date is then recorded when the next instructional prescription is introduced (see Figure 24B).

In addition, it is extremely important that the tutor maintains a very accurate record of his or her daily tutoring activities. This is done by recording the appropriate information (the date, the time spent on various activities, a description of the tutoring activity, and what the student learned as a result of the activity) in the Tutor Log. The tutor should make a separate entry in the Tutor Log for each activity even if more than one tutoring session occurs on the same day (see Figure 25).

4B. Maintain Additional Records for Younger Students

If the student who is being tutored is younger than 12 years of age, the tutor should maintain a Contingency Record as well as send a daily Progress Report home with the child. Information regarding these two records is found in the preceding chapter of this book. Even though these two records are not used with older students, the tutor should frequently take time to discuss the student's progress with him or her.

Step 5: Review the Student's Progress

5A. Review Instructional Prescriptions
Previously Learned

One of the most severe deficiencies in the traditional classroom is that once stimuli are learned by the student, they are not systematically reviewed. Consequently, as a result of not consistently using newly-learned information or skills, the student forgets within a short time much of what he or she has learned. This problem can be overcome to a great extent if the student is provided the opportunity to

Figure 24A

Example of Mastery Date on Profile Sheet

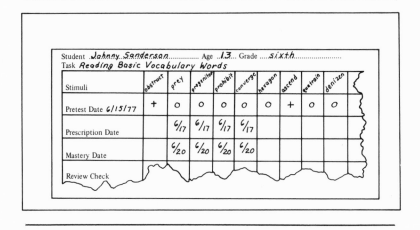

Figure 24B

Example of Next Prescription Date on Profile Sheet

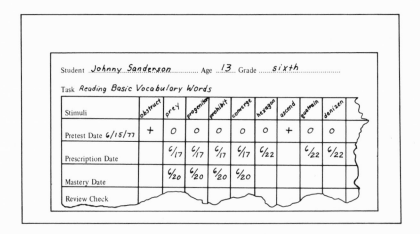

Figure 25

Example of Various Activities on Tutor Log

Date	Time	Description of Activity	Comments
6/17/77	10 min.	had Johnny rehearse the following words: obstruct, prey, progenitor, prohibit, converge.	he spoke very softly and was timid
6/19/77	5 min.	rehearsed the words: obstruct, prey, progenitor, prohibit, converge.	he started to speak louder
6/19/77	3 min.	checked the student for learning.	Johnny knew the words "obstruct" & "prohibit"
6/20/77	10 min.	introduced the word "converge" and drilled Johnny.	

systematically review or use what he or she has learned. Furthermore, it is very critical that this review is not left to chance. After a student successfully learns a specific instructional prescription, the tutor should do the following:

1. At least once a week, place one flash card for each previously-learned stimulus in a stack. Have the student respond to these stimuli independent of the specific instructional prescription on which he or she is currently working.

2. Have the student respond in this manner to previously-learned stimuli for a period of at least four consecutive weeks from when the stimuli were first learned. In other words, if the tutor were working with a student systematically over a period of time, he or she would be reviewing numerous instructional prescriptions previously taught, in addition to working on a current instructional prescription.

3. If a student is unable to respond correctly without

hesitation to a previously-learned stimulus, the stimulus should be included again in subsequent instructional prescriptions.

4. The tutor should make notations in the Tutor Log each time a previously mastered instructional prescription is reviewed. The tutor should especially note any stimuli with which the student has difficulty.

5. Approximately every four weeks, the tutor should make a formal review check and record the student's performance on the student's Profile Sheet. This entry is made by recording the date in the upper portion of the square in the "Review Check" column, and a plus (+) or zero (0) in the lower portion of the square. Plus (+) designates a correct response and zero (0) designates an incorrect response (see Figure 26).

5B. Administer the Delayed Posttest

The tutor cannot assume a student has mastered a particular instructional outcome just because he or she gives an immediate correct response. True mastery has not been achieved unless the student is able to demonstrate mastery at least three months after he or she first demonstrated mastery of the instructional outcome.

For example, in the course of the school year, the tutor should posttest a student to measure his or her mastery of previously-learned stimuli at least three months after mastery is achieved. If possible, the tutor should have someone other than himself or herself administer the posttest. The person administering the posttest should observe the following procedures.

Option 1
• Use the flash cards when posttesting a student.
• Tell the student how he or she is expected to respond when the flash card is presented (e.g., "When I hold up a flash card, tell me what sound the letter makes.").

Figure 26

Example of Review Check on Profile Sheet

Task **Reading Basic Vocabulary Words**

Stimuli	obstruct	prey	progenitor	prohibit	converge	hexagon	ascend	quatrain	denizen
Pretest Date 6/15/77	+	O	O	O	O	O	+	O	O
Prescription Date		$^c/_{17}$	$^c/_{17}$	$^c/_{17}$	$^c/_{17}$	$^c/_{17}$			
Mastery Date		$^c/_{20}$	$^c/_{20}$	$^c/_{20}$	$^c/_{20}$	$^c/_{20}$			
Review Check	8/11 +	8/11 +	8/11 +	8/11 +	8/11 0	8/11 +	8/11 +		
Review Check									
Posttest Date									

- Say, "Tell me the correct answer if you can. If you do not know the answer, say 'I don't know.' "
- Do *not* tell the student the correct answer.
- Hold up one flash card at a time.
- If the student is able to answer correctly, *do not* say anything.
- The person administering the test should place each flash card face down in front of himself or herself.
- Make a record of the stimuli to which the student responded correctly.

Option 2
- Reproduce the test that was used as a pretest and use it as a posttest.
- Follow the testing procedures specified for administering the pretest (see Step 1B).

• Under "Posttest Date" on the Profile Sheet, record the results of the posttest as administered. A plus (+) is recorded under each stimulus the student was able to respond correctly to without hesitation and a zero (0) under each stimulus to which the student either failed to respond, responded incorrectly, or hesitated before responding correctly (see Figure 27).

If the student is not able to respond correctly to every stimulus on the posttest, and if the stimuli are critical to the student's subsequent success in a given subject, the tutor should continue to work with the student on those stimuli with which he or she is still having trouble.

Applying the Structured Tutoring Model to Other Content

If someone intends to apply the Structured Tutoring model to types of learning other than stimulus-response, he or she should follow the five basic steps outlined in this chapter. However, caution should be taken to ensure that the testing and teaching strategies are appropriate for the specified objectives. Obviously, flash card drills will not be appropriate for other types of objectives. The reader can see from the examples discussed in this chapter how carefully the tutoring techniques have to be specified to ensure the student will benefit from the tutoring experience. The authors have found that the specific tutoring techniques and procedures corresponding to each type of instructional objective are refined only after a great deal of formative evaluation and revision of the materials. (The term "formative evaluation" is used here to describe the process used by the authors to obtain data for the purposes of increasing the efficiency and effectiveness of the instructional materials.) Therefore, if someone attempts to apply the Structured Tutoring model to instructional tasks other than stimulus-response, extreme care should be taken to include an intensive formative evaluation process. If the reader is interested in examining tutoring procedures and materials that correspond to objectives which

Figure 27

Example of Posttest for Profile Sheet

Student .Johnny Sanderson.......................... Age ..13... Grade ...sixth......

Task Reading Basic Vocabulary Words

Stimuli	obstruct	prey	progenitor	converge	hexagon	ascend
Pretest Date 6/15/77	+	O	O	O	O	+
Prescription Date		6/17	6/17	6/17	6/17	
Mastery Date		6/20	6/20	6/20	6/20	
Review Check	8/11 +	8/11 +	8/11 +	8/11 O	8/11 +	8/11 +
Review Check	9/15 +	9/15 +	9/15 O	9/15 +	9/15 +	9/15 +
Posttest Date 12/7	+	+	O	+	+	+

are not stimulus-response in nature, he or she should refer to the list of materials provided in the "Resources" chapter of this book.

Summary

In this chapter, we have focused on the specific tutoring procedures and techniques that apply to stimulus-response learning. It was emphasized that though the strategies and procedures outlined in this chapter can be applied to stimulus-response learning tasks in general (naming letters, producing sounds, reading words, identifying symbols, etc.), the specific strategies are not appropriate for other types of learning activities. In addition to the general procedures and techniques presented in Chapter II, the five steps of the Structured Tutoring model were discussed: (1) preassess the student's present ability; (2) prepare to tutor the student; (3) tutor the student using the proper tutoring techniques and procedures; (4) maintain the appropriate records; and (5) review the student's progress.

IV.

OUTCOMES

In the previous chapter, the five steps of the Structured Tutoring model were discussed as they apply to stimulus-response learning tasks. It was emphasized, however, that Structured Tutoring materials have been developed to meet the more complex learning needs of students in reading, math, and second language instruction.

Since the inception of the Structured Tutoring model in 1967, an extensive amount of research has been conducted in an effort to validate the Structured Tutoring reading materials. In the 1975-1976 school year, for example, over 200 school districts throughout the United States implemented the Structured Tutoring reading program and compared the results with their former remedial programs. Success was clearly indicated after evaluating individual learning gains of students, responses from tutors and teachers, and parental feedback.

The data collected from these evaluation efforts suggest the following outcome: Reading deficient students progressed an average of two to three grade levels in one semester, representing a rate four to nine times faster than had previously been experienced.

Aside from significant gains in reading grade level, the data gathered from the evaluation efforts suggest other important outcomes of the Structured Tutoring reading model:

1. The students tutored showed a remarkable change in attitude toward school. A large majority of students who received tutoring experienced a positive change in attitude and got along better with their classmates. In many instances, the students tutored enjoyed reading for the first time.

2. The students tutored retained their skills after returning to the educational mainstream.

3. According to parents of the students who received tutorial help, their children are now more interested in reading; they read more at home and are better readers from supplementary books.

4. According to parents of the students who served as tutors, their children demonstrated observable growth in social skills. The parents felt that this growth was important enough to warrant their children missing other subject matter in school so they could serve as tutors.

5. The students who served as tutors demonstrated improved reading ability as a result of overlearning and reviewing basic reading skills.

6. In many instances, the right to serve as a tutor provided sufficient motivation for hard-to-discipline students to the extent that they changed much of their negative behavior.

7. School principals reported very few difficulties with the Structured Tutoring reading program and that disruption of classrooms to permit individualized tutoring was minimal. The principals stated that the gains made by most students in reading were outstanding enough to outweigh any organizational difficulties.

8. Teacher time and effort were reduced and supervision of students needing remedial help was facilitated.

9. The amount of learning obtained per dollar for each student far exceeded the amount previously expended to remediate students.

10. It is important to note that many of these outcomes suggested by the Structured Tutoring reading program agree

with the data collected in math and second language Structured Tutoring systems.

Summary

The data suggest Structured Tutoring is a viable complement to traditional instructional techniques. The data collected from the many studies similar to the examples discussed in this chapter continue to show that trained nonprofessionals, as well as paraprofessionals and professionals, can produce significant results for students of varying age groups across a variety of instructional objectives (reading, math, stimulus-response tasks, etc.). Yet, it is surprising that the majority of educators in most schools to this point in time have virtually left untapped the human resources available to them. One possible explanation for this fact is that the educators, for the most part, do not receive the appropriate training in this critical area.

References

Droegemueller, L. (Assistant Superintendent of Schools). The Function of Data in Identifying Subjects and Assessing Program Impact. Rosemount School District #196, Rosemount, Minnesota, May, 1977.

Evaluation Report: High School Tutor Project. Northwestern Utah Service Center, n.d.

Final Report: Jordan Tutorial Project. Jordan School District, Salt Lake City, Utah, July 8, 1974.

Harrison, G.V., J.C. Wilkinson, and D.C. Clark. Effects of a Tutoring Program in Reading Remediation—Eighth-grade, Glendale Junior High School, n.d.

Osguthorpe, R.T., and G.V. Harrison. Parents: A Potential Instructional Resource for the Public School. Paper presented at the California Educational Research Association Convention, Los Angeles, California, November, 1973.

Progress Report: Utilization of Instructional Assistants for the Development of Reading Skills. Cardston School Division #2, June, 1974.

For a comprehensive list of studies evaluating effectiveness of Structured Tutoring programs, contact: METRA, Box 1000, Blanding, Utah 84511.

V.

DEVELOPMENTAL GUIDE

The Structured Tutoring model is characterized by (1) a precise tutor-student relationship and (2) highly structured instructional materials. To ensure an effective tutor-student relationship, tutors must be trained so that they are totally conversant with both the general and the specific tutoring techniques discussed in this book.

The general tutoring procedures and techniques are discussed in detail in Chapter II: "Operational Description." The proper training of tutors should involve extensive interaction with all of the general techniques and procedures. This training should be accomplished through proper explanation and modeling on the trainer's part as well as sufficient involvement of the tutor in directed role-play situations.

The specific tutoring techniques and procedures are integrally related to the nature of the desired instructional objectives. Generally speaking, there are five basic steps in the development of Structured Tutoring materials. Figure 28 lists the five steps for applying the Structured Tutoring model to instructional objectives. While these five steps have been discussed in detail in this book as they apply to stimulus-response learning tasks, they are applicable given critical modifications to other instructional objectives as well. For example, as outlined in Step 2, the preparation of instructional materials for stimulus-response objectives only

Figure 28

Applying Structured Tutoring to Stimulus-Response Tasks

STEP 1:   Preassess the student's present ability
           a. Select appropriate instructional outcomes
           b. Prepare a record of the student's progress (Profile Sheet)
           c. Prepare a pretest
           d. Pretest the student
           e. Record the student's performance on the Profile Sheet

STEP 2:   Prepare to tutor the student
           a. Prepare instructional materials (flash cards)
           b. Prepare a record of daily tutoring activities (Tutor Log)
           c. Specify instructional prescriptions

STEP 3:   Tutor the student using the proper tutoring techniques and
           procedures
           a. Follow general tutoring techniques and procedures
           b. Follow specific tutoring techniques and procedures

STEP 4:   Maintain the appropriate records
           a. Maintain the Profile Sheet
           b. Maintain the Tutor Log
           c. Prepare and maintain a Contingency Record (for young-
              er students)
           d. Prepare and maintain a daily Progress Report (for
              younger students)

STEP 5:   Review the student's progress
           a. Systematically review instructional prescriptions pre-
              viously learned
           b. Administer the delayed posttest

---

involves the preparation of flash cards. Obviously, one would not use flash cards to accomplish more complex instructional objectives. For example, to meet the instructional objective of successfully transferring basic reading skills, the flash card procedures discussed in this book would be utilized to teach the stimulus-response tasks associated with reading (letter names, letter sounds, sight words). However, reading consists of a great deal more than mere stimulus-response learning.

The authors have developed a variety of manuals based on the Structured Tutoring model as it applies to more complex learning objectives. A general perusal of these manuals will demonstrate to the reader the wide diversity of instructional strategies which accompany the more complex learning objectives. If the reader is interested in developing instructional materials that go beyond the scope of the stimulus-response task, or if the reader would like to collaborate with the authors in developing instructional materials which address more complex learning objectives, he or she is encouraged to contact the authors. In addition to the manuals and materials listed in the "Resources" chapter of this book, the authors are currently developing instructional materials to meet other educational and training needs.

VI.

RESOURCES

Since the inception of the Structured Tutoring model in 1967, the model has been applied to a wide range of subject matter and audiences. In many instances, the tutorial systems or manuals are not available commercially. The purpose of this chapter is to provide the reader with a concise summary of instructional and training materials that are available. In addition to the Structured Tutoring materials listed herein, Home Study courses are available from Brigham Young University for several of the Structured Tutoring manuals. These courses are designed to train a person to use the various manuals. For example, Education 514R Section 23 is designed to train a person to use *Beginning Reading I.* The credit can be used for recertification in most states, and many colleges and universities will allow those registered to apply the credit toward an advanced degree.

For persons who are not interested in enrolling in a home study course for the purposes of obtaining recertification credit, self-training packages have been developed to accompany the reading, mathematics, and second language Structured Tutoring manuals. Completion of the self-training packages can, at a later date, be transferred to home study courses, if desired.

If a group wants to learn how to use a particular manual, a member of the group may request that a training workshop be conducted in a convenient location.

For further information regarding home study courses, self-training packages, and group training workshops, write or contact:

METRA, A Division of Utah Navajo Industries
P.O. Box 1000
Blanding, Utah 84511

**Manuals and Materials Based on
the Structured Tutoring Model**

Title	Subject Matter	Designed Use
I. READING Beginning Reading I	Basic reading skills	To be used by an adult to teach children between five and nine years of age basic reading skills.
Beginning Reading II	Advanced reading skills	To be used by an adult to teach advanced reading skills to children between seven and 12 years of age.
Basic Reading for Secondary Students	Basic and advanced skills of secondary students	To be used by a person 15 years old or older to teach students, between 13 and 18 years of age, basic and advanced reading skills according to individual needs.
Basic Reading for Adults	Basic and advanced reading skills for adults	To be used by an adult to teach adults reading skills according to individual needs.
Supervisors' Guide for the Basic Structured Tutorial Reading Program	Basic reading skills for children between five and seven years old	To utilize older students (ten to 12 years of age) as tutors for children between five and seven years of age.

(Continued on Next Page)

Manuals and Materials Based on
the Structured Tutoring Model

Title	Subject Matter	Designed Use
Supervisors' Guide for the Advanced Structured Tutorial Reading Program	Advanced reading skills	To utilize older students (ten to 15) as tutors for children between eight and ten years of age.

II. MATHEMATICS

Title	Subject Matter	Designed Use
Beginning Math I	Basic math concepts covered in the kindergarten, 1st, and 2nd grades	To be used by an adult to teach a child between five and eight basic math concepts in kindergarten, 1st, and 2nd grades.
Beginning Math II	Basic math concepts covered in the 3rd, 4th, 5th, and 6th grades	To be used by an adult to teach a child between nine and 12 years of age the basic math concepts for his or her grade.
Supervisors' Guide for the Structured Tutorial Math Program	Basic math concepts covered in kindergarten, 1st, and 2nd grades	To utilize older students (ten to 12) as tutors for children between five and eight years of age.
A Structured Tutoring Guide for Teaching Math Facts	Addition, subtraction, and multiplication facts	To be used by an adult to teach children, between seven and 18, math facts.
Teachers' Guide for Training Students How to Teach Themselves Math Facts	Addition, subtraction, and multiplication facts	Provides a teacher or aide step-by-step procedures in how to train students how to teach themselves math facts, and how to maintain a record of the facts learned by each student.

(Continued on Next Page)

**Manuals and Materials Based on
the Structured Tutoring Model**

Title	*Subject Matter*	*Designed Use*
Supervisors' Guide for the Structured Tutorial Math Facts Program	Addition, subtraction, and multiplication facts	Utilizes students as tutors to teach peers or younger students math facts.

III. LANGUAGES

Title	Subject Matter	Designed Use
Beginning English I	The basic grammatical structures of the English language	To be used by a person who speaks English and the student's native language to teach the student English.
Beginning Spanish I	The basic grammatical structures of the Spanish language	To be used by a person who speaks English and Spanish to teach someone else Spanish.
Beginning French I	The basic grammatical structures of the French language	To be used by someone who speaks English and French to teach someone French.

IV. GENERAL

Title	Subject Matter	Designed Use
Five Steps to Successful Tutoring	Stimulus-response tasks other than math facts, such as letter sounds, sight words, etc.	To be used by an adult tutor (15 years of age or older) to teach stimulus-response tasks to students between four and 18 years of age.
How to Organize an Intergrade Tutoring Program in an Elementary School	The procedures for selecting, training, etc., of student tutors and the procedures for testing, etc., the children to be tutored	To be used by a teacher or aide who wants to utilize 4th, 5th, and 6th graders as tutors for primary-grade children.
How to Be an Effective Tutor: A Handbook for Secondary Tutoring	Techniques and procedures for tutoring secondary students	To be used by an adult to tutor secondary students. (*Note*: It is assumed the tutor is very knowledgeable in the subject matter.)

(Continued on Next Page)

Manuals and Materials Based on
the Structured Tutoring Model

Title	Subject Matter	Designed Use
How to Be an Effective Tutor: A Handbook for College Level Tutoring	Techniques and procedures for tutoring college-age students	To be used by a college student to tutor another college student in any subject matter. (*Note*: It is assumed the tutor is very knowledgeable in the subject matter.)

V. SPANISH LITERACY

Aritmetica Inicial-Guia del Tutor	Basic Mathematics for Spanish-speaking students	An instructional guide used to teach a person the basics of arithmetic: addition, subtraction, multiplication, and division.
Escritura Inicial-Guia del Tutor	Basic Writing for Spanish-speaking students	An instructional guide the tutor uses to teach basic mechanical writing skills.
Lectura Inicial-Guia del Tutor	Basic Reading for Spanish-speaking students	An instructional guide the tutor (teacher) uses to teach basic reading skills to Spanish-speaking adults or children on a one-to-one basis.

GRANT VON HARRISON is a Professor in the Department of Instructional Science at Brigham Young University. He received his Ed.D. (1969) at the University of California at Los Angeles with a major in instructional product research. For the first year of his training, he was involved in W. James Popham's product research training program, and for the last two years of his training he was associated with System Development Corporation (SDC) and the Institute for Educational Development (IED). It was at SDC during the summer of 1967 that the Structured Tutoring model evolved. Since that time, Dr. Harrison has conducted numerous research studies based on the model, in which a variety of populations have served as tutors. Dr. Harrison has developed intergrade tutorial systems and has authored and validated various manuals for adult tutors as well as instruction manuals for organizing an intergrade tutorial program in an elementary school. Dr. Harrison joined the Graduate Faculty at Brigham Young University in 1969.

RONALD EDWARD GUYMON directs the world-wide literacy program for the Church Educational System of the Church of Jesus Christ of Latter-day Saints. Previous to his current position, he was an Assistant Professor in the Department of Instructional Science at Brigham Young University. He received his Ph.D. (1977) at Brigham Young University with a major in Instructional Psychology. During the three years of his graduate training, he worked extensively with Dr. Grant Von Harrison on applications of the Structured Tutoring model, including exportable self-training packages and a unique second language instructional model. During the last two years of his graduate training, he worked as a consultant to numerous school districts in several states. In addition, Dr. Guymon served as the manager of the Department of Research and Development for Media, Education, Training (METRA) with the branch in Orem, Utah.